AN EXMOOR CHRISTMAS

AN EXMOOR CHRISTMAS

Compiled by
Steven Pugsley

HALSGROVE

First published in 2000 by Halsgrove
Text © 2000 Steven Pugsley

ISBN 1 84114 096 1

British Library Cataloguing-in-Publication-Data
A CIP data record for this book is available from the British Library

HALSGROVE
Halsgrove House
Lower Moor Way
Tiverton EX16 6SS
T: 01884 243242
F: 01884 243325
www.halsgrove.com

Printed and bound in England
by MPG Books Ltd, Bodmin

Contents

Introduction

An Exmoor Christmas. Does it deserve to be marked out or recorded above any other observance of the Festival? Can it really be any different to the celebrations, indulgence and excess experienced anywhere else in Britain at the dawn of the twenty-first century – or, indeed, anywhere else in the world in these diminishing days of global media and commercialism?

The answer, I believe, is an emphatic yes. Christmas on Exmoor is distinctive – perhaps unique – and certainly special. Part of it may be something to do with the climate for few would deny that Exmoor has *real* weather. December can bring a palpable change in the air, the tingling frost and skitter of snow that means that the Moor is one of the few places in England that with some frequency experiences a genuinely white Christmas. More often, the Christmas holidays are the prelude to a long and harsh winter and tales of blizzard and blow are an inextricable part of the Exmoor experience.

Like many remote communities, Exmoor preserves a strong sense of its traditions, be it carol, cookery or ceremony, and a recurrent theme of many writings about the place – old and new – is how vital and tenacious these customs are. The daily round of the hill farm has altered little in essence over the centuries and the great turning points of the year are marked with no less veneration now than they ever were: the symbolism of new life springing from the darkest days of winter is never lost on a hard-pressed Exmoor farmer. Exmoor, of course, is sheep country and the concerns and tribulations of the shepherd on our windswept uplands are at heart no different to those of the shepherds abiding in the field two thousand years ago. And so when we sing that 'The first Nowell the angel did say, was to certain poor shepherds in fields as they lay', there is in many Exmoor people a little bit of unconscious pride that it was our kind who heard it first.

There is about the place a strong feeling of that sort of bridge between the present and the past, and sometimes the ancient past at that. The most potent symbol of Exmoor, the Red Deer, figures in a rich winter mythology, pagan and Christian, and – again – when the carol tells of 'The rising of the sun and the running of the deer' the Exmoor identification is pointed. But above all, Exmoor is a land of old and enduring faith, certainly from the days when the Celtic

Saints struggled ashore from the Bristol Channel to spread the Gospel, and perhaps earlier. For there is a legend that Christ himself came to Exmoor. The story goes that as a young man Jesus set forth on a trading expedition with Joseph of Arimathea (who in time would return to plant his thorn-blossoming staff at Glastonbury). A tremendous gale drove their ship on to the beach at Glenthorne. Joseph and Jesus set out to find fresh water and, failing in the quest, Christ miraculously caused a spring to rise which flows to this day.

Christmas on Exmoor has a real meaning. No one would deny the delight in the gift or the fun of a good party. But here there is more to it than the material. On Exmoor the *spirit* of Christmas survives.

The compiler feeding his winter flock, Molland, 1964.

So the Year Moves on to Christmas

From *Wild Harvest*, 1978

HOPE BOURNE

Hope Bourne is the doyenne of Exmoor writers and from her home in the heart of the Moor has observed the approach of Christmas for more than forty years. In Wild Harvest *she sets the scene.*

So the year moves on to Christmas. The great mid-winter festival, part pagan, part Christian, is no-where more well-kept or more rejoiced in than here in the hill-country. Though beasts must be fed and stock looked-to as usual, no-one does more work about

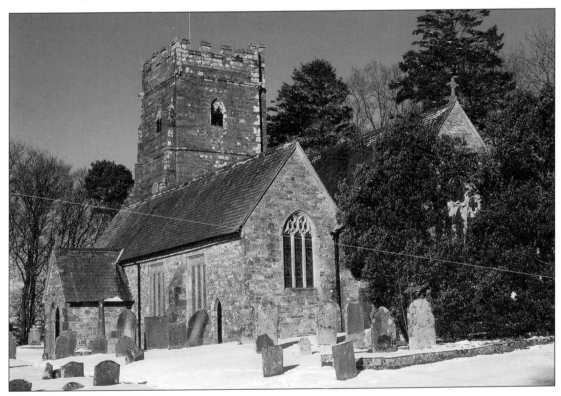

St Mary Magdalene, Exford.

E.R.J. Davey

the farm than is necessary over the fortnight that covers Christmas. It's a time of high days and holiday before real winter sets in with the New Year. There's the tying of presents, the decorating of rooms – even I bring in holly and fir to deck my little home and set up the gay cards on my shelves – the baking of cakes, the preparing for parties. There's the Carol Service with the Church all embowered in Christmas greenery and children reading the Lessons. There is Midnight Mass, with the Church windows glowing out into the darkness of another Christmas Eve, and another Christmas Morning when we come home again. There's Christmas dinner with families gathered together, there's the Boxing Day Meet when the quarry most hunted is that out of a bottle and the Boxing Day shoot when it's marvellous if anything's shot. There's parties and dances and whist-drives, and comings and goings all over the place. Oh, what a wonderful time is Christmas! (And if it lasted any longer we'd all be dead of overeating and exhaustion!)

New Year's Eve is the final fling of the festivities (except for those of us who remember Twelfth Night). Now it is the long haul through to the spring, with the endless rounds of caring for the beasts and battling with the elements of rain, wind, snow and ice.

The Village School in Winter

CICELY COOPER, 1979

We have promised ourselves a late ride in autumn to see the lovely beech hedges and variegated greens of the woods. In the event it was a very late ride. We met the snow going up Ley Hill on to the top, and at Stoke Pero it was an inch deep. Great bursts of cloud rolled across and swept round Dunkery enveloping it in a thunderous purple blue and the Hangmans were pencilled out against a faintly lemon band of light.

We decided to stay on Exmoor and go no further than North Molton. At Landacre the Barle was roaring and flooding. The only spot that seemed sheltered enough for a picnic, was the very grim Valley of Rocks, deep brown, partly snow-covered, but with a little trapped sunshine gleaming invitingly on its landward slopes.

We had enjoyed every glimpse of the villages straggling up the hillsides, softened with snow mantles, and with that shut-door look, betokening warm fires and blue wood smoke going up, and swirling down on the north-west wind. I glanced at the 'closed forever' village schools and my mind went back to the early years of the century, when there was abundant life therein. No car transport – and children dressed for the open air! Unconcernedly they would come tramping up, knock the snow off boots, shake their coats, and rush madly for the stove, which had better be glowing or boys would see to it that it was.

In one hill school I knew, their joy was an open fire grate, with hobs, and thereon, the milk and kettles sizzled. Outside, was abundant joy in the form of unswept snow. Ink and water was frozen – it is true, but what need of indoor entertainment? The kitchen was beset with problems, but the fire roared – the good smell of roasting and baking issued from it, and steaming cups of coffee and tea. What use for lessons? As it neared Christmas, the chief delight was to venture forth into the frosty country in search of holly and evergreens. Back the bundles would come, and busy, fully occupied pupils would seize and decorate all the hoops and gloriously hang the sparkling results from the beams. The school would smell like a pine forest and then the foresters would bring up the tree.

This had to be secretly decorated overnight, and adorned with individual packages, addressed to each pupil. All day before the feast, knocks would be answered on the back door and mysterious parcels would come in. These unwrapped were, cream, trifles, cakes and – in the kitchen, what was much preferred, sandwiches of salmon and sardines, were piled up on plates always emptied first when the time came. The stage must go up – the Nativity costumes came forth and be refitted. The star – the manger – the stable objects, including animals, and excitement would mount. Every child had a part to play and every parent would be expected to come and appreciate the performance.

The school, for those weeks, with its fun and games, its comradeship and close contacts, the help given by the older to encourage the less initiated, the decided good will to the teachers and desire to assist instead of resist – oh! what a loss was here, to the village, when it no longer resounded to school children's enthusiasms. The church, the parson, the squire and the parishioners all enjoyed the event together as a family.

So I looked at the silent village schools, and reflected that the 'good old days' really were as good as we are sometimes accused of imagining. Whatever advantages have been obtained, that which has been lost is of a different order which may not, in these days, fit the newer patterns. But it was the life of the moor and its roots go deep.

Christmas at Allerford

From *Memoirs of Selworthy and West Somerset, 1951*

CICELY COOPER

I have mentioned that some festival doings were always afoot near Christmastime in the School. The war did not greatly affect our keeping of the feast because everybody gave of their utmost to make the children forget and to treat the evacuees. We began preparing a play in November. Quite often we had a Nativity play and this gave us great scope for learning some of the wonderful carols I used to hear in Harrow when Dr Percy Buck and Mr E. C. Broadhurst produced such supremely lovely carol services and entertainments in the Speech Room and at the old Church on the Hill. I taught some of my able singers Dr Buck's own carols and even the very rare ones, that with such exquisite taste Mr Broadhurst searched out for his boys at Harrow. The Allerford children and some of the evacuees quickly picked up and appreciated the strange tunes, and it kept them very busy fitting the carols into scenes of the play.

Mr Thomas, of course, used to put up the stable and took as much interest in this as in Maypoles. A manger – oh yes! he would soon make that. He only drew back pausefully at a donkey. No! he didn't really see that he could produce cattle – but we did have a donkey's tail once, and we always had a good lamb. The boys were the shepherds and kings – the girls were the angels and how they loved their butter muslin wings. They learnt immense scripts and endless verses of carols, and on the great day all the kind friends of the School were invited to attend. The children looked eagerly for their parents and I tried to learn to know a few of these on the rare occasions when I met them, for this was the primary purpose of the gathering. But some friends I did know and I might be excused if, like the children, I looked eagerly for them.

Two Managers I haven't before mentioned, because they were not present at the original meeting I have described. But we hardly ever had an 'occasion' at School to which Mrs. Hughes and Lady Pilcher did not come. Mrs Hughes was sometimes described as the School's Fairy Godmother. Very many gifts she gave us, as did other ladies in the parish, but none so welcome as her actual attendance at our concerts and hearty enjoyment of the same. It did us a great deal of good to see the pleasure our quaint performance gave, nor can I think of a school function without Mrs Acland. These were Managers who gave just that human support and personal interest that is lacking in big schools where the managers are officials only. There came a time when Mr and Mrs Cosford left Selworthy, and we greatly missed them, too, at a school concert. The family party was never quite the same, though Mr Evans, the next Rector, followed in the tradition of former incumbents and always came to our functions. He once entered into a shinty match, waving a walking stick manfully and smiting the ball to the children's delight – but this is a summer event, not a Christmas one.

Much labour as the Nativity plays involved, they were not really half so successful as one we did, called 'Mother Shoe,' or 'Cinderella,' mentioned above. In the former we had the inimitable performance of a very largely made boy, one Timmy Robins. All the Robins children had character, and Timmy had a memory to learn the script easily. He was 'Tom Tom' and he stole the pig and howled to perfection. The sight of him hiding behind a 'Mother Shoe' half his girth was enough to send the actors into fits of laughter, to say nothing of the audience. Timmy Robins made a deal of swashbuckling noise in the School, but we lost one who was just cast for characters of outstanding humour when he left.

I had thoughts of running 'Toad of Toad Hall,' with Timmy for leading role!

In 'Cinderella' we had one of the most perfectly beautiful little girls I have ever taught, to my thinking. She had a round apple blossom face with an aureole of curly golden hair and vivid blue eyes overshadowed by dark lashes. She was very petite in stature and we dressed her up in a real old-fashioned lace dress that I think had once been Mrs Acland's in her youth. We adapted it – high waisted, puff sleeves – blue sash and sequins, and she was a perfect beauty of the early Victorian times – a really fine Cinderella. She was just eight years old and had the unsophisticated grace of fairy tale age. Afterwards we made her Selworthy's Queen for the National Savings Week, and she went to the Regal Theatre at Minehead to be admired. Her Prince was a curly haired boy with Irish blue eyes, distinctly roguish in expression – not quite the pantomime prince, but well enough. And the ugly sisters – we had the best laugh out of them, of course – but you would hardly think a tiny village could produce professional scenery. Well, it did. For there lived at the time there a young lady who had come for her health and simply revelled in scene painting, which she knew professionally. I cannot say how many hours Miss Herring and her two friends put in at night painting on the floor, ballroom scenes, star spangled skies or the shoe house. But the result was to turn a dull school room into a veritable Christmas wonderland. Excitement rose high when the carpenters of Holnicote put up the stage and threw into the porch great loads of evergreen and holly which, being the property of the National Trust, we were not allowed to pick ourselves.

The children fell on them and for a day or two the room was like a fairy tale wood, heavily scented with bay leaves and firs, which the children wove into garlands and hung everywhere. Then up went the coloured bells and silver chains. Everybody was on steps and as seriously busy about it as if there were no war raging. I have said that Mrs Harris was a wonderful caretaker. I cannot imagine how we could have held any of these high jinks without her continual practical resourcefulness. I directed operations like a general, but the practical working out of plans was devised by Miss Floyd and afterwards Miss Main, the children and whenever anyone could not think of what to do next, Mrs Harris was requisitioned and invariably solved any difficulty with strong practical commonsense.

Let us not forget either the School Secretary, who, in the midst of her accounts, was called upon to fix up stage lighting or adjust scenery. She had at one time cooked and baked for our feasts and no one looking at the Christmas tea would ever have thought of war or rations. The smell of puddings and cakes filled the air for some days. The fire roared and children would steal down to look at the array of tarts and watch the icing being made. Each cook we had produced her own specialities. I remember Miss Chard for her jellies and lovely savory sandwiches. It would be hard to say which cook made the most marvellous icings with snowmen, sledges and other oddities, but Mrs Slape lit an array of candles, and this produced an indescribable 'Oh!' on the part of the children. There were gifts of cream, too. Holnicote provided a large tree and the Assistant Teacher and I scoured Minehead for gifts to hang on it. It looked resplendent enough ablaze with candles and silver paper, but I must say that the toys for which we paid high prices were very poor compared with those which hung on trees in our youth. Alas! where were the fairy dolls and cuddly bears, trains, &c.? The children seemed delighted enough with those we bought. Yes, of course, Father Christmas was brought in to give them away. This event is never quite received as grown-ups expect it will be. Silence and solemnity greets his sallies – something like fear. Who is it? Is it the Rector? Someone creeps behind to have a better look. No! it isn't! Well, who then? They decide to look brave and laugh anyhow.

Then we used to give ourselves over to the traditional noisy games for 'all who will' and off home, cuddling toys, to 'Auld Lang Syne.' Then we grown-ups look at the debris of another Christmas at Allerford. We did our little best to clear up, but thank goodness there was a Mr and Mrs Harris.

The Holly Bears a Berry

From *A Moorland Year, 1993*

HOPE BOURNE

The holly bears a berry as red as any blood...' and so does this dark December day. The holly tree at the top of the wood on the precipitous cleeve bears a load of scarlet such as one would scarcely believe were it painted in a picture.

It is a tall tree, full-grown, and rises high above my head, holding its crown of splendour brilliant against the grey sky of the shortening Winter afternoon. No bush ever bred or cultivated by Man the gardener can match the wild holly for the profusion and spectrum-redness of its berries, nor does any other tree set off its fruits with such massed deep-green shining foliage. As I look up at the beautiful tree that rises so royally here in the depth of the winter, amongst the bare-branched thorns and scrub-oaks, I notice what a clever tree it is: up to a height of about 7 or 8 feet it bears the needle-spined prickly leaves we know so well; above this height, the approximate limit of animal browsing, it dispenses with such armament and grows only plain smooth leaves. How many generations of trial-and-error, of natural selection, have taught it this ploy? I speak with respect to her – it is a she-tree, for only the female bears the berries – and take just a few sprigs for my Christmas decoration.

There are many hollies in various states of growth, in and about this and other woods, and in the hedge-bank, for the holly is a native tree in these parts, growing naturally in company with oak, ash and hazel. Testimony to this is given by a number of places having received the name of Homebush, holm or home being the ancient name for holly, no doubt once prolific in these parts.

The Surprises of Decemeber

From *Wild Exmoor Through the Year, 1930*

E.W. HENDY

Winter, amid the moors and coombes of the West, is a time of happy surprises; for thanks to the mutabilities of our inconstant climate, it is the unexpected which always happens. In some years the mellowness of autumn lingers on till within a week or two of a green Christmas; you may find herb-robert, mallow, valerian, periwinkle, forget-me-not, campion and scabious – even a late foxglove – and a dozen other common flowers in bloom in the hedgerows. A sprig or two of bell-heather is always to be seen in some sheltered corner. Gorse is ever in flower. I have seen a lady-bird amid its spikelets in November, and have found primroses in my hedge before Christmas.

To mankind, winter sunrises are more familiar than those of summer. We wake to find the room flooded with a subdued rosy radiance; above the rim of skyline streaks of tawny orange and glowering red sprawl like the glistening length of some gaudy dragon-salamander. Pines top the ridge in silhouette; below them the still darkened moorland shades from purple into velvety black; the arc above is packed with ruffled clouds, tinged with infinite delicacies of rose, from the faint blush of apple-blossom to the carmine of flamingo's wing; between them are rifts of metallic blue, unfathomably deep. And across this riotous pageant of colour rooks and jackdaws, tossed and buffeted by the wind, steer their clamorous journey to feeding grounds on emerald meadows by the sea's verge.

The country folk describe such a memorable dawn more succinctly; they say 'The reds are out,' and prophesy rain before evening. Often they are right, but it may portend only wind. In any event a change in the weather follows, soon or late. The next morning you may look out upon a dazzling wonderland of snow. The moor, all its rugged contours smoothed and softened, seems to have drawn nearer during the night, so clear and vivid are its outlines. With glasses, or even with the naked eye, you may see a line of black specks crawling downwards over Robin Howe towards the woods which fringe the coombes; they are the red deer seeking the succulent ivy which clothes the stunted oaks; walk through any sheltered woodland and you will find the ivy leaves bitten off as high as a stag can reach, upright on its hind legs: if the snow lasts, deer become so tamed with hunger that they scarcely move at your approach.

On the meadows near the sea, where the snow lies but sparsely, and vanishes most quickly, birds, driven from more northern latitudes by stress of weather, congregate in multitudes – finches, waders, gulls, plover, and thrushes of all species. But the ravens and the rest of the crow tribe still haunt the moorland wastes: deep snow may mean dead sheep, and where these are the carrion eaters are gathered together.

Walking one morning after a blizzard, I took a pathway which led me down into the Horner Woods, and in a moment I was in a fairy land. Each crinkled branch of stunted oak was limned in snow, and where a cluster of dead leaves had given the flakes a resting place the laden branches were bent and curved; from ancient oaks and alders which clothe the lower slopes the unwonted burden had ruthlessly torn great limbs. Halting some thirty yards down the path I looked back along an alley completely arched over with crystalline tracery, and at the end of the vista was a glimpse of a glistening waste of moor, rising gently to a sky of a very pale and filmy blue.

Tales of cars and lorries embedded in snowdrifts on the moorland roads led me the next day to climb Porlock Hill and see for myself. As I trudged upwards I began to think that perhaps the stories were exaggerated; the half-thawed surface was slippery, but until I reached the one thousand feet line the snow was only an inch or two deep. A two-seater car, containing two

Porlock Hill in the 1920s – clearing a way for Lynton Visitors.

Exmoor Photographic Archive

cheerful motorists, passed me about half-way up. But, once on Porlock Common, there was a change. Soon I heard the two-seater grunting and groaning; as I came round a corner I saw it endeavouring to back out of a drift. Eventually its efforts were successful, and it retreated whence it came, with the occupants perhaps a trifle dashed in spirit. Drifts began to cross the road, first one, then two, and at length three feet deep. Soon it became impassable. I had hoped I might penetrate as far as Oare Post and enjoy that wonderful prospect over the heart of Exmoor. I persevered for another half-mile, and then had to give it up, for now the snow was over my knees.

Retracing my steps, I met another fellow-creature whose intrepidity put the two motorists to shame. He had pushed a bicycle, to whose handlebars was attached a bass bag which contained a turkey, up the thousand odd feet from Porlock. And he proposed to traverse some ten more snowy miles to Lynton. I did my best to dissuade him with dismal tales of cars buried in unfathomable depths at Lillycombe and Culbone Stables, and pointed to a darkening sky which looked ominous. But, unpersuaded and indomitable, he decided to continue his trek. Whether he spent the night in a snowdrift, his head pillowed upon the turkey and stags nibbling at his frozen whiskers, I cannot say. If my sanguine traveller ever reached Lynton he deserved to enjoy his Christmas dinner; it was well-earned.

Christmas Customs

From *The Book of Exmoor, 1903*

F.J. SNELL

On Midsummer Day, while it is chiming twelve, a maiden will pluck a full-blown rose, blindfolded, and wrap it up in a sheet of white paper. This she refrains from opening until Christmas Day, when, according to some, it will be found as fresh as when she gathered it. Better still, if she puts it in her bosom, the young man she is to wed will come and snatch it away.

Miss Alice King has made this custom an excuse for a charming picture of West Country life:

'But why is sweet Bessie, the farmer's dark-eyed daughter absent from her merry companions? She is sitting in yonder deep window-seat, where the moonbeams are falling softly on something she holds in her hand, while her cheeks burn and her heart beats. Let us steal across the room, and take one glance at that object which she touches almost reverently as her fingers close lightly over it. It is a withered rose. For some time Bessie has loved handsome Robin, the young Exmoor farmer, whose uncle is her father's neighbour, and there seems some reason to believe, by certain signs and tokens known in the silent alphabet of lovers, that her affection is returned. But Robin is a very shy wooer, and Bessie, like all West Country maidens, is very proud and reserved, and therefore the courtship languishes.

'Thus it has come to pass that Bessie has hit upon an exceedingly original way of making her backward suitor declare himself. Long ago, in the bright summertime, she gathered a blush rose on Midsummer Day, and stealthily, secretly, so that not even her mother could know, she laid it carefully in the inmost recesses of her drawer. She has thought of that rose all through the golden harvest weather, and dreamed of it at night, and now, on Christmas Eve, she has taken it out of its hiding-place, and tomorrow she will go to church with her withered rose in her breast. Robin is paying a Christmas visit to his uncle, and Bessie fully believes that if in reality he loves her, he will be compelled by the virtue of that charmed, withered midsummer rose to go up to her when he meets her on Christmas morning, and take it from her bosom, and this will be an infallible sign that his heart is hers, and they will be married before another Christmas Day comes round.'

An allusion has been made to Christmas as the time to which love-sick maidens look forward with eager anticipation. But, of course, they are not alone in this. From the gleeful children who chant the quaint carol beginning

> Christmas Day in the morning,
> Joseph whistling, Mary singing,
> All the bells of heaven are ringing,
> Christmas Day in the morning

to the old folks who sit and warm themselves by the ashen faggot on Christmas Eve, all regard the holy season with high approval and satisfaction. Even the beasts of the field, it is said, are aware of its approach, for in every cowshed the 'master-bullock' – i.e. the finest and strongest of the cattle – will low three times at the first stroke of midnight, and then go down on his knees before the manger, as if in homage to the Babe of Bethlehem. No master or mistress allows servants or labourers to work on Old Christmas Day – that is, if their employer is wise, since the infraction of this rule is apt to bring with it the direst consequences. Miss King relates the following story of a 'terrible near woman,' whose love of money tempted her to break the time-honoured custom:

'On the morning of Old Christmas Day, instead of putting on her best dress and bonnet, and going to church, as all West Country good Christians do, she put on her second-best bonnet and her thick grey cloak, and had the horse harnessed and put into her tax-cart, and drove to the nearest market town to sell her butter and eggs, of which she took good stock with her in the cart, neatly packed in two or three baskets. All went well with the dame at first. She disposed of all her wares in the most satisfactory way, and at a high price. The inhabitants of the town, as she went from door to door, appeared to have a special liking for the produce of her dairy and poultry-yard. It was Christmas-time, and everybody was anxious to secure good cheer for their families, and certainly in all the neighbourhood there was no such butter and thick, solid cream as the dame's – there was no denying it.

'At length, late in the afternoon, the dame started homeward, with her purse well filled and her baskets empty. It had been a beautiful winter's day, and she jogged along in much placid comfort and contentment, counting up her gains in her mind. At dusk, however, a thick fog came suddenly on, after the fashion of fogs near Exmoor, and the dame began to have much trouble to see her way in the dark lanes; but she was what is called in the West Country 'a spurrity woman,' and she kept on her way undaunted. She was within half a mile of her home, when her little horse, who had Exmoor blood in him, all at once started violently, upset dame, cart, and baskets, freed himself from his harness, and galloped home without them. The dame

Wassailing at Carhampton, c.1950.

was picked up with a broken leg, from the consequences of which she limped all her life after. The conduct of the horse was attributed to supernatural intervention.'

In connection with Christmas, it may be mentioned that in the West Country it is reckoned a crime to kill a robin. This notion is believed to have sprung from a beautiful old legend that, as the Saviour hung on the cross, the little bird toiled to extract the nails from His bleeding hands, and that some drops of sacred blood, falling on its breast, left the red stain which we now find.

On the 17th of January, the eve of Old Twelfth Day, it is customary to sing to the apple trees and fire off guns, in order to ensure a bounteous crop. This practice is not absolutely confined to the West Country, though it is probably more generally observed here than in other parts of the kingdom. The ceremony, which is known as "wassailing the apple trees," is thus per-formed: A party of labourers, with whom perhaps is the local Vulcan or carpenter, makes the round of the orchards, starting about seven o'clock in the evening, when the men have left work. In each orchard that they enter a ring is formed, and then the quaint wassail song, of which the words are traditional and doubtless of great antiquity, is sung by the assembled band. As might be anticipated, there are different versions of the ditty in different localities, but the variations are comparatively slight. Thus in some places the first verse commences –

> It is our wassail round our town,
>
> Cup it is white, and ale it is brown.

This unlooked-for allusion to ale seems at first very singular and out of place, and does not occur in all the renderings of the song. The word 'wassail,' however, which is derived from the Anglo-Saxon *Waes-hael* ('Health be to you'), formerly denoted a liquor composed of apples, sugar, and ale, which was greatly in request at carousals. It may be added that the term – pronounced in the West Somerset dialect 'wazzayal' – is now only heard in connection with the custom of singing to the trees. After each verse the leader shouts in stentorian tones –

> Hats full, caps full, three bushel bags full!
>
> Hip, hip, hip, hurrah!

And the others join heartily in the acclaim. 'Formerly,' says Mr W. Elton, 'an old musket was brought round and discharged at each hurrah; but of late years this has been wanting, the men perhaps not being willing to risk the vigilance of the officers of the Inland Revenue.'

Mr Elton is, we are sure, quite mistaken, if he means it to be inferred that the custom of firing at the trees has fallen into desuetude. It is certainly as common as – our own impression is, much more common than – the habit of singing to them. Labourers, it is true, no longer carry muskets or fowling-pieces, as they did once; but in most districts there is no lack of guns, and the farmers and their sons are, many of them, quite superstitious enough to provide against the omission of the ceremony. One line of the song explains 'And a little more cider will do us no harm.'

This is evidently intended as a hint, and in the hospitable farmhouses of the West Country such a hint is invariably acted on.

'A bucket of hot cider, with toast floating on the top, is now,' says Mr Elton, 'sent out by the owner of the orchard, be he squire or farmer; the toast is placed in the apple trees for robins to eat, while the cider lubricates the throats of the singers. They form a curious and picturesque sight, these men in their rough working clothes on a bright and frosty night, with the moon shining down through the bare and rugged branches of the apple trees on their scarcely less rugged features; and if by chance there be a few inches of snow on the ground, the effect is perfect. One forgets that it is the end of the nineteenth century, and you fancy yourself assisting at a Druidical function of the dark ages. The whole company then march up to the back entrance of the house, singing a verse which ends with the line –

So open the door and let us all in.

Upon which knocking is heard, the door is opened, and the men come in. More cider is supplied, and dancing is indulged in, usually to the accompaniment of a somewhat asthmatic accordion; if the maid-servants of the establishment are many and comely, the visit is often prolonged. Cheers for the family bring the visit to a close, and the men troop off to go through the business again at the next orchard. It is astonishing that many of the older men really believe that if this custom were omitted, a poor crop of apples would assuredly follow; and, if a man is unpopular, his orchard is purposely avoided.'

As all who have had experience of such matters are aware, nothing is more difficult than to secure a connected version of a rustic song. Almost invariably one's interlocutor can remember snatches, like the lines already quoted, which serve to convey an idea of the composition, but even when pieced together, do not represent the whole. So far as our knowledge extends, the only extant copy of the wassail song that can be deemed authentic and trustworthy, is that furnished by Dr Prior, of Halse, to the Rev. Wadham P. Williams, of Bishop's Hull, who, in turn, communicated it to the *Somerset County Gazette*. It is worth quoting, as the Exmoor version, which may yet be recovered, must have closely resembled it.

Wassail, wassail, all around the town;
The zidur cup is white, and the zidur is brown.
Our zidur is made from good apple trees,
And now, my fine fellows, we'll drink, if you please;
We'll drink your health with all our heart,
We'll drink to ee all before we part.

  Here's one, and here's two,
  And here's three before we go;
  We're three jolly boys all in a row,
  And we're three jolly boys, all in a row.

This is our wassail, our jolly wassail,
And joy go with our jolly wassail.
Hatfuls, cupfuls, dree basket, basketfuls
And a little heap in under the stairs.

Down in a green copse there sits an old fox,
And there he sits a-mopping his chops.
Shall we go catch him, boys – say, shall we go?
A thousand to one whor we catch him or no.

There was an old man, and he had an old cow,
And for to keep her he couldn't tell how;
So he bild up his barn to kip his cow warm,
And a liddle more liquor'll do us no harm.

And now we'll go whooam, and tell our wife Joan
To put in the pot the girt marrow-bone,
That we may have porridge when we do cum whooam.

There was an old man, and he lived in the West,
The price of a barrel wur what he loved best,
He loved his old wife so dear as his life,
But when they got drunk, why, they soon cum to strife.

The Ashen Faggot

From *Somerset Birds, 1943*

E.W. HENDY

The burning of the ashen faggot on Xmas Eve is still observed on Exmoor and at least by one family in Porlock. A friend has given me a description of the ceremony in which he has often participated. It is a family affair and the whole household assembles in the kitchen. The faggot is of green ash, five or six feet long and two or three feet in depth. It is tied round with withy bonds and placed on the open hearth upon the top of the cinders. It burns until morning and the heat is so great that you have to hold a newspaper before your face. As each bond breaks there is a drink of cider all round; hence bibulous families tie many bonds. (Teetotallers prefer cocoa.) Every person in the room sings a song or tells a story, or recites.

The Ashen Faggot is consigned to the flames in Dunster.

The ceremony has obvious affinities with the Yule Log: the custom was on Xmas Eve to light a heavy block of wood, called the Yule Log, together with a fragment of its predecessor that had been kept throughout the year for that purpose. Authorities differ as to whether this rite had a solar origin or was purificatory: if the former, it was a piece of imitative magic. Like the Midsummer fires, it was intended 'to them ensure a needful supply of sunshine by kindling fires on earth which mimic the source of heat in the sky'. Naturally Midsummer and Midwinter, the times when the sun's heat begins to wane and wax, would be the appropriate times for these kindlings.

In *Somerset* (Cambridge County Geographies) it is stated that the Ashen Fagot Ball, a festival long kept up at Taunton, was believed to commemorate that chilly night when the soldiers of King Alfred found, to their joy, that green ash branches made excellent camp fires. But the similarity of the rite to the Yule Log ceremony suggests a more ancient origin. It is perhaps significant that Ygdrasil, the tree of life in Scandinavian mythology, is an ash.

The Ashen Fagot

From *Echoes of Exmoor,* First Series, 1923

At Christmas play and make good cheer, For Christmas comes but once a year.
Tusser: *Farmer's Daily Diet.*

The burning of the Ashen Fagot in North Devon on Christmas Eve is one of the most ancient and beautiful customs amongst us; and I am urged by the Club to write about it as it was observed around Exmoor during the last century, before it passes away altogether into that forgotten past whither so many beautiful customs are heading apace amidst the hurly-burly of modern ways. It is a pity that all memories of it should die, even if the practice does, for I am told that there are only a few yeomen left in North Devon who burn the fagot in the proper olden manner since coal-fires and kitchen ranges (called here Bodleys) have replaced the old hearthfires and made the ashen fagot a thing of the past. And it is held by the old people that this has had its due effect upon the spirit of joviality and friendly conviviality which once possessed all classes alike at this season of the year.

I will therefore take the reader to one of these old manor farms where the custom is still observed just as it was a century ago; we will help cut the wood, bind it together and bring it in, and sing and play and talk and laugh around it as it burns – giving a place also to those touches of sentiment and sympathy (and therefore sadness) without which the joy of good friendship and good fellowship becomes somewhat hollow and unreal. One old rustic moralist with whom I was often talking, till he died, told me that at these parties there were always one or more who sang sentimental songs, or told tragic stories, or recalled events of the past loaded with sadness or horror, and he added that it was in accordance with the 'viddiness of dthings,' that it should be so; and before the art of fiddle-playing had declined in our neighbourhood there was a fellow called Boundy, who did not know a note of music, but who could extemporize on his instrument till the party laughed with joy or wept for sorrow of heart. I have often thought that Tennyson's stanza of wild joy beginning with 'Ring out wild bells into the wild sky' derives its peculiar power from its setting in the resigned and thoughtful sorrow of the 'In Memoriam.'

This year a few members of the Club were invited by Farmer Ridd to spend the Christmas Eve at Severn Barton and help to burn the Ashen Fagot, and I was among them. I arrived about mid-day, to find a party of men gathered about a magnificent ash tree growing in the corner of one of the fields. It was a glorious December day and the sun shone brilliantly with almost horizontal rays across the landscape throwing deep long shadows of every object in its light. There was also that crispness in the air which foretold a cold night, when the Christmas fire would burn with a blue inner flame merging into red and white. We all worked hard with saw, axe and hook, till the 'beans' were bound about the fagot-wood and the logs of 'hard-wood' cut in proper lengths, and all was loaded up in the long carts and the teams started home at a merry pace. When the huge fagots and logs had been placed conveniently within reach of the Great Hall fire-place, the men dispersed to prepare themselves for the feast.

Severn Barton is built in the Elizabethan style, with a huge hall and wide hearth fire-place, a massive beam across the top carrying an overmantel of carved oak. A few smouldering embers were there in readiness to light the fagot as I came in with other friends. A large Cromwellian table ran from end to end of the hall, with seating room for forty people, bedecked with viands of every kind – a round of beef, a haunch of venison, two very large hares, a turkey and a goose to match, a brace of ducks and another of pheasants, were noticeable among other smaller dishes. Four men entered soon after carrying the huge fagot of ash bound with chains, followed by others with logs saying as they did so that the party were all there except one 'Alf' and he was 'like th'ole dowg's taale always behind.'

The fagot remained for a minute hissing and spluttering on the coals, with the whole party standing round it, and then up it crept in little lambent flames crackling and snacking as they rose, each nearing the other till they merged into one broad fiery mass which roared and leaped till it reached some eight feet high and filled the whole hearth with its upward stream of burning gas lighting up and warming the Great Hall and the ruddy-faced and laughing guests. The burning of the ashen fagot had begun.

On this occasion there were present not only the farm hands themselves, but all their families, excepting the children still at school. They were all turned out in their best, and the difference in dress and general deportment between those of to-day and those of a century ago is only what might reasonably be expected as the result of compulsory education and higher wages. Simplicity is in all classes the essence of good company, and the Exmoor labourer is not yet 'spoilt,' if he ever is to be. But there is a growing tendency towards more conversation at such feasts – more desire of each to take a simple part in entertaining the rest, and certainly a marked progress in ability to do so. That accounts for the varied programme which was to follow. But the actual supper went off quietly, almost silently, for we have not risen yet to that ideal of a meal in which Pope says:

St. John mingles with my friendly bowl
The feast of reason and the flow of soul.

In order to make Exmoor people talk in an assembly of hearers, it is necessary for one – usually the Host or Chairman – to draw each one as we 'draw' a cover for a stag. He speaks in a resonant and loud but kindly voice, and addresses each person in turn, asking a question or giving a playful thrust at his guest. It happens this year that Farmer Ridd had won the Champion Cup at Smithfield Show with a fat Devon ox of his own breeding, and the cup after supper was filled with champagne and the health of the herd and breeder was drunk all round. Ridd's brother George was there, whose failure in life and farming has been as conspicuous as his brother's success, and it appears he is glad now to work upon his brother's farm, where he does pretty much what he likes. Asked by the proposer to support the toast, he took a deep draught from the cup and then said: 'Ees, yer's ole Jack he'th a-bin up to Lunnun an' a-win'd this yer Cup, an' he'th a-bin tu every place – An' yer be I, I've a-bin tu no place – an' – an' I'm 'swell 's e is !!'

Another guest called Bale, when appealed to to say how he liked the cup replied: 'I didn' look 'tic'ler tu the Cup, but the stuff Maaster 'th a putt in to 'n – I wish me droat was a mile long zo's I could taaste it all way down!'

H. Hole

Christmas Fatstock Market at Dunster, c. 1907

In this way – with an occasional word from the host or other prominent person addressed directly to a guest – the supper was punctuated by repartee followed by bursts of laughter and short crafty comments. At length supper was ended and all drew round the fire in a semicircular row and prepared to enjoy each other's company to the full. Each guest was asked in turn to supply something. Farmer Ridd led off with 'The Farmer's Song,' the chorus of which was:

> Come gather around my fagot to burn
> Come gather around said he
> Here's Jack and here's Jill – they have worked with a will,
> So Christmas right merry shall be!

A String Band accompanied the songs when the melody was not too original. This band is the result of enthusiastic efforts of a member of the Club to revive instrumental playing on the Moors. In olden times each parish had its string band – that was before the invention of the harmonium, terrible in all its forms. So the 'Farmer's Song' being well-known was accompanied by the string band, and the chorus was done with wonderful power.

Amid the silence that followed, one old Dick Hepper burst in with a loud voice, jumping up in his place: 'I've a zeed ighty Chursmases! I've a zeed Ighty Chursmases! I've a zeed ighty Chursmases!' (He always said three or four times what he wanted to say.) 'Then you must be eighty years of age Mr Hepper?' said Farmer Ridd.

'No I bant, bant ighty – I be only zeventy-nine! But a zeed Ighty Chursmases !'

It transpired that he was born on Christmas eve seventy-nine years ago. Roars of laughter greeted the discovery of the riddle, and as they died away the old man resumed his seat murmuring as he did so 'I've a zeed ighty Chursmases – I've a zeed ighty Chursmases.'

At this juncture Jack Crascombe came out with his well-known song:

A 'APPY-GO-LUCKY OLE CHAP.

> Chorus – A 'appy-go lucky ole chap
> No matter what pace I do go
> I yer the volks zay
> He be merry alway,
> Can't zee why't should'n be zo.
>
> I was born in a rare lucky time,
> Last year of the cen'try an' all,
> The last month and day, hour and minute volks zay
> Else I never should been born at all.

A mewlin' and pukin' young brat,
I crawled out of bed for a lark,
Valled flat on me back and killed a gurt rat
Who was aitin a' me mulk in the dark.

When older they putt me to schule
To taich me vor raid and vor write,
The more of the schulle the bigger the vulle
All I larned was to swear and to vight.

Zo they putt me to work on the varm
To larn vor to plough and to zow
Couldn' go a lot varder, vor even me vather
Couldn' tell me what I didn't knaw.

Vor sport I can tell 'e a tale,
Wan morning' I walked 'cross the Bray
It made me quite shiver when out of the river –
Me' boots vull o'trout vit to vry.

Up 'cross the Gurt Meadow I went
Climbed up a tall bank wi' me hands,
With each of the pair I gripped a gurt hare
I'm tellin' 'e just as it stands.

I got to a round Barly rick
Wi' pigeons all thick on the thatch,
Twist me gun round me lags, and shut round the dags
Zo killed all the birds wi' one scratch.

I nex' bought a varm wi' no cash
Wi' timber drawed in as an ort
Timber then went up top, and I cut down the crop
An' zo had me ole varm for nort.

I've lived yer vor all me long live
A merry go lucky ole chap
No man's enemy – no man's friend d' 'e zee?
Zo write me this yer epitap!

EPITAPH.
I was married when ighty an' ight
Just ninety-and-nine when I died – o!
An' now I don't care, vor I've had all me share,
Zo fel-de-del-diddly-i-do

This rollicking song, well-known around Exmoor, brought out some more humorously 'tall talk' from the guests. One thought to beat some of its canards by a story that his father's employer grew such big swedes that when an old Exmoor ewe and lamb were lost on the farm they were discovered peacefully chewing their cud within the rind of a succulent root which they had excavated for themselves! Other great things followed, each with its chorus of laughter until a confused hubbub of talk ensued and no one's voice could be heard for some time. To control these extravagancies I offered to show some simple tricks in sleight of hand, which had the effect of steadying the spirits and restoring a certain amount of silence. Then the 'Reverend' told his 'Short Story' which was compressed into eight words:

Boy-Fun!
Toy-Gun!
Gun bust!
Boy dust!

This was laughed at quietly, with less boisterous comment. Then he put it into Latin (post classicé), thus:

Ludum, agitas, pupille
Gaudium das, fusille;
Fusille rumperis, heu!
Pupille, pulvis tu!

A very few of us invited guests were amused at this, but the rest sat still and wondered.

But 'the Reverend' seemed afraid lest we with a little knowledge of Latin should take this translation too seriously, and he went on to give us a classic version:

En puer! En ludus! nova gaudia sulfur et acer
Clangor, et audaci machina pulsa manu
Me miserum! propria tuba vi dispergitur; eheu!

Qua tuba reliquice; qua puer ante, cinis!

All this tended to reduce the spirits of the rural guests still further. Not a word or sign showed anything but blank amazement, and stillness reigned in the hall once more. This was what the parson apparently desired, for he at once announced (at a sign from the host) that he would now tell his untold and true Ghost story – an event which happened in an Exmoor Rectory. It was listened to with profound silence, and no remarks were made at its close, except a suggestion that the scene was at Knowstone Vicarage or Charles Rectory, and after a few moments of reverie, the band commenced softly, in calm pathetic strains, the accompaniment to a song by a tall young farm-worker called Mark Coles, whose tastes and abilities lead us to think of him as the future Poet of Exmoor. He has also a beautiful baritone voice and sings his songs to music composed by a friend in Barnstaple.

The music stopped a moment while he told us that this also was a true thing that happened in his own family about a hundred years ago.

Dulverton, c1912

Exmoor Photographic Archive

COMING HOME.

Hearts were merry, hands were busy
On the Eve of Christmas-tide:
Steps were lightsome, faces gladsome,
Round the old farmhouse fireside.
For that evening home were coming
Sisters – brothers from afar.
All were singing, bells were ringing,
And the old door stood ajar.

Hearts were heavy, eyes were weary
On the Eve of Easter-tide:
As they gathered they had whispered
'Tis the worst that could betide.
For above us father, mother,
Both lie wrapt in endless sleep,
And the corpse of yet another
Rocks upon the cruel deep.

Years then passed and all were gathered
To an early resting-place,
Save the sailor who was harboured
On an island, where our race
Never trod until the surges
Dashed him on the level sand.
There he lived till wandering pilot
Brought him to his native land.

Hearts still merry, hands still busy
On the Eve of Christmas-tide:
Steps still lightsome, faces gladsome,
Round the old farmhouse fireside.
But time's changes had brought strangers
In the place of loved ones gone.
All unconscious he approaches –
Learns it now is others' home!

So again the sailor wanders
Now for choice is once for need,
And on that old Christmas ponders
Welcoming each storm with greed;
For he says, when the Last Wreck comes
It will be upon the strands
Of the Island of the Lost Ones
Where Life's Captain calls 'All hands!'

This song marked the climax of sentiment and pathos in the evening's programme. Soon the party came back again to the usual Christmas-tide temper, and in that strain the evening continued to its close. The old game of Truckle-the-Trencher lasted on to the morning, and then the simple country dance and 'Auld Lang Syne' broke up the circle. Meanwhile, the ashen fagot, replenished over and over again, had been burning before us. Sometimes its heat was so intense that seats were moved back, and as it cooled down we came forward again. All the fire-bricks and the hearth were white and the chains holding the original fagot were hanging loose and red hot. Refreshments were passed round, consisting mostly of hip-top ale and cider, but there was no tendency to excess, save in a solitary case, and that was watched over by one or two with wily discretion and care.

Farmer Ridd's successful and benevolent face beamed with delight as we took our leave; but as I crossed the threshold I heard his old brother George addressing him in a tone a little out of harmony with the spirit of such an evening: 'I say Jack! gi us a quart o' zider to draw into me zistern vor I be got mortal dry!' I thought of the proverb about the skeleton in the cupboard, as we wended our way across the moors on that beautiful frosty Christmas morn. 'Well,' said my Reverend companion in answer to my protesting ruminations, 'I suppose this also belongs to the Exmoor "viddiness of dthings!"'

Christmas at Cutcombe

From *Home Chimes*, 1891

ALICE KING

First of all, let us step into the old grey village church; the door is open, for the ancient sexton is doing what he calls 'putting up the Chrismassing'. The December twilight comes on apace, and the whole building is unpleasantly suggestive of ghosts, but the old man says quite cheerfully, 'If there be any spurrits here, I ban't gallied at them,' and he puts on a jaunty, not to say familiar air, as he talks of such spectral visitants. For all head-gear he wears a red handkerchief curiously knotted and arranged around his head and face, and he looks very much as if one of the gargoyles round the tower has just come to life and stepped down from its usual elevated situation.

The hand of the architectural restorer has not yet touched this church; the high pews are like so many commodious loose boxes for captured Exmoor ponies to take their ease in; the east wall is pierced with a quaint little square window, and above the pulpit there is a strange, canopy-like erection, called a sounding-board. There is no want of Christmas decoration, albeit of no aesthetical and artistic style. The church looks as if a small neighbouring plantation of evergreens had just walked into it. Old Mat, as they call him in the village, has 'put up his Chrismassing' to a purpose; from every corner and cranny blooms forth a branch, even from the half-broken hand of the crusader who lies on the monument in the southern aisle. Scarlet berries are hanging in rich profusion; though they are twined into no elegant wreath, they climb up to the centre arch, where is displayed that curious old picture of Moses and Aaron, Mat's joy and pride; they fringe the front of the gallery, where tomorrow the Christmas anthem will ring out with a will from clarionet and bassoon, without any weak assistance from St Cecilia and her organ-pipes. That Christmas anthem will be, in truth, a wonderful and unique production in the musical way. How will the choir roll forth the prolonged notes, how will the melody wind in and out and twist itself into marvellous turns and trills, how will the words return again and again until the heads of the listeners will almost be giddy with the complex evolutions of sounds. The faces, too, of the Christmas choir will be a study worthy of a Rembrandt in their solemn, absorbed, ecstatic enjoyment of their own music. Old Mat will lead the strain, and he will be sure to be equal to the occasion; he and his fathers before him have sung that Christmas anthem, for it is impossible to say how many years and generation after generation in the church have listened to it in rapt admiration.

And now the most important West-Country custom, indispensable on Christmas Eve in every properly constituted West-Country farmhouse, is at hand. The door of the kitchen is opened wide, and the oldest labourer on the farm walks majestically in, carrying a huge ashen faggot on his shoulders. No West-Country farmer would have any good luck throughout the coming year if the ashen faggot was not duly burned in his house on Christmas Eve. The faggot – which is a goodly load of wood, such as might be a respectable burden for a Spanish mule crossing the Sierras – is set on fire with much pomp and circumstance in the broad hearth; there is a furious crackling and snapping of the branches, and a roaring of the blaze up the wide chimney, such as might reasonably arouse uncomfortable fears in a nervous guest, and the Christmas family bonfire is burnt with peals of riotous laughter, and merry jests, and brisk volleys of fun, among young and old, master and men, mistress and maids, together.

The most favourite amusement of the young people in the West Country is dancing. They are as fond of it as the French peasantry when they dance at the festivals of their chosen village saint. These West-Country dances are always danced around the Christmas ashen faggot. As we sit in the settle corner, we mark with pleased eyes the natural, untaught grace of the girls as they weave in and out through the often complicated figures of the strange, old-fashioned West-Country dances. There is one dance, called the 'Handkerchief Dance', which is a perfect silent poem, as the girls with their partners – fine stalwart young fellows, whose limbs have been knit together and braced by many an Exmoor breeze – pass and repass, and raise their arms, and sink almost on their knees alternately, and form themselves into a changeful, living web of movement, ever recurring, and yet not one moment the same.

Among the elder folk there is much handing round of 'cobler's punch', a West-Country mixture of cider and gin, and much singing of songs. These songs are many of them very quaint as to words; the two most characteristic, perhaps, are a song, the chorus of which imitates all the noises made by the different animals on a farm, the whole party going into the performance when the chorus comes round with right good heart and will; and a song which glorifies the good qualities and useful properties of the horned Exmoor sheep. The songs are interspersed with Christmas carols, some of which are very ancient and curious, and the music of which has never probably been printed, but lives in the minds and hearts of the people alone, re-echoing on from Christmas to Christmas, backward and backward, until, as we strain our ears to catch the sounds, they are at length lost in the murmur of the waves of time.

The Crosshand Dance

From *The Witch of Withyford; A Story of Exmoor,* 1896

GRATIANA CHANTER

It was a sharp Christmas that year, I mind. There was a heavy snowfall on the Friday and then the frost set in, and the roads was all to one glidder making it properly difflcult to get about.

The river was frozen over down to Ford, a thing the oldest liver scarce could mind, and as rarely happened, by reason of the quick running of the water.

The young folks liked the cold, making slipper-slides, and having games with the snow, and finding it an easy job to track the rabbits and birds. But it was a bad job for the dumb creatures and they as looked after the sheep, and those who were old and whose blood crept slow in their veins; sure for them it was terrible bad!

To be sure, I mind that Christmas well; and many's the times when sitting quiet here, I look a long ways back and think deep on the hows and whys of things. For Bill Crocombe and me was courting then.

We used to walk together in the lane at the bottom of Grange Gates, and sure 'twas mortal cold. But sweethearts be sweethearts all the world over, and weather, and wind, and rain, don't make much difference to them, so long as they've got each other.

'Twas so with Bill and me. I'd just put mother's old shawl over my head and then out to meet him down by the Linhay so soon as I heard his whistle. For there was often more company in the Grange kitchen than they who were courting cared much about, and sweethearts have things to say, and ways as they don't want the whole world to know.

I can mind every bit of the road as if those walks were taken but yesterday. How the trees were all to one sparkle and glitter, and the moors rolling off and away in great drifts beyond the sooty oakwoods in the hollow.

The stars above were just as bright as the frost below, and all was wonderful still. And how our breath went up like steam from a kettle, and the smell of frost in the air.

There were forty red-deer as came down every night to the cleve across the Combe. Bless you!

they wouldn't have come so nigh to Withyford if it hadn't been mighty cold out over and the fodder uncommon scarce.

'Twas on Christmas Eve, and just such a night as I've been telling of, as all Withyford was met together in the great hall up to the Grange, for dancing, supper, and such like. The young master he was down, and nought would please the old one, but as all the folk should come up there to make merry, and enjoy themselves, by way of keeping Christmas.

'Twas mostly left to mother, but her was a clever one to manage, I can tell you, and sure, the supper looked splendid, laid out on tables the whole length of the kitchen.

'Twas about seven o'clock when they started the dancing. They put Jimmy Crick on the table in the window, and there he sat with a jug of ale beside him (for they do say as fiddling be terrible thirsty work), and there he sat a-tuning up, and screwing of his fiddle, and telling to Johnny Light, as to what dance they'd have. For Johnny Light, though crippled and pummel-footed too, was a proper man to set the dancing going, though the one to dance off all the lot was Billy Coats the chimney-sweep, my! he could go!

The old Squire was up at the higher end of the hall, close against the fire, and the young Squire stood beside him. They were telling with some of the old folk, Farmer Jan, and Farmer Will, amongst the number. The old Squire's hair showed white against the black oak of his chair, and his eyes, for all the world like a hawk's, were shining brighter than I'd seen them for many a year.

Ah Lord! poor soul! 'twas no wonder they'd grown dim!

And the young Squire, bless him! why, you could hear him laugh from one end of the hall to the other, it did one good to hear him. And sure, he was a beautiful man to look at, as he stood there on the hearth with his golden curls a-shining in the light, same as the time when mother carried him into that very hall, nigh fifteen years agone, though now he was six feet two, and as broad across the shoulders as Dick the blacksmith.

'Twas a pretty sight that Christmas party up to Grange. For 'tis always pretty and full of life, where men and maidens meet with a wish to enjoy themselves, and the old folk by, to see there b'aint too much foolishness.

The men and maidens were all forming up for a crosshand dance, and showing out plainly against the dark oak walls. They took some time making up their minds as to what partners they would choose, and Joan Richards for one had refused three or four, as thinking Jan Williams would ask her. But Jan was another way about.

Mother was in the kitchen, just patching up a goose with a bit of parsley (as the cat had taken a bit out of it, through the door being left open), when Jan Williams he put his head in and saith quick and eager like,

'Where be Malvina hiding to?'

'What do'ee want to know that for?' mother answered sharp, 'her don't want ye courting her in the dark, when you won't speak to her in the light like a man. I'd be ashamed to behave like that there to so fine a maid, if I was you, Jan Williams,' mother saith.

Jan Williams he looked at mother straight, and shut his lips tight. He was a fine black-eyed, black-haired boy was Jan, and well set up. He had a look on his face that night, mother saith, as if he'd made up his mind to do something, and do it he would, and 'twould be a strong man as would turn him from his purpose. She noticed too that he was pale in the face for him, and slighter than he used to be. 'Sure he's in earnest about Malvina,' her thought to herself.

'Tell me where the maiden be,' saith Jan, 'and then I'll promise you Thirza, that both you and Withyford shall see afore long, why for I want her.'

'Lord!' saith mother, with a sneering laugh, as if her didn't believe him, 'then that will be something new I warrant. Well, she's out in the passage there; but she won't thank me for the telling.'

Malvina was up at the higher end of the passage, peeping through the little window that looks into the hall. She was standing on tiptoe watching the folk inside. The passage was long and dimpsey, except right under the window, and she was so taken up with what was going on that she never knew as Jan Williams was nigh till he was right close upon her, and sure, then her jumped with fear.

'Don't ye be a-feard,' he saith, ''tis only me. Thirza, she said you was here; I was wanting you and asked. Though she reckoned,' he saith bitterly, 'as you'd soon have my room as my company.'

Malvina she turned round, and lent with her back against the wall under the window, so as the light fell on her lovely curls, and her face was in the shadow, but not so much as Jan couldn't see every bit of its beauty, nor the haughty look in her great eyes, as she looked straight at him.

'What do you want me for?' she said.

'To dance,' he saith.

Malvina lifted her brows and looked prouder than before.

'With who ?' she asked.

'With me,' saith Jan.

Malvina keped her wonderful eyes on him while he stood there, poor lad, with his face white and working; for he was as strung in love with her as a man can be, and her coolness near drove him mazed.

Malvina held up her hand, and marked off each word with her finger.

'*You* want me to dance with *you*,' her saith; '*you*, Jan Williams, afore the whole of Withyford parish, to dance with *me*, "Malvina, the Witch's Maid!" Do you know what you're telling? Jan Williams.'

And she threw back her head and laughed, a little bitter sneering laugh, as showed her pearls of teeth, and the whiteness of her throat, but weren't a happy thing to hear from the mouth of a maid.

'Malvina, you don't believe me,' he cried!

''fore God I mean it!'

And then, I suppose, she saw he did, for her cheeks flushed up and her eyes flashed, and her saith, slow and thoughtful-like,

'Jan Williams, you be a brave man, and I like you for it. I most surely do.'

'Like me,' he cried with his eyes upon her, 'Oh Malvina, sweetheart, why I love you, I love you, and there's nought upon this earth that I wouldn't do for you! Listen and hark to what I'm telling, Malvina!'

Just to that moment Jimmy Crick he struck up with his fiddle, and the folks started inside with the crosshand dance. Jan had hold of both Malvina's hands, and in another moment he'd have had his lips on her's, but with a quick twist she loosed herself from him, and down the passage she flew like a bird, and where the full light streamed in from the hall door, she waited a moment for him, with her finger on her lips.

'Now,' she whispered soft, while her eyes shone and her breath came quick 'Now Jan, be you ready to take the consequence?'

He just looked down at her and took her hand tightly within his, and led her right into the hall.

They'd begun the crosshand dance at the bottom of the room. Johnny Light, he was capering about fine. 'Twas strange how active he was to be sure considering how whirlfooted he was. Jan he led Malvina through the room thinking to get her into the dance quiet without no notice being taken; but that weren't to be.

No person could see such a couple as those two, a-coming along hand in hand, without taking two looks at them. Malvina had on her dark stuff dress, with a red handkerchief about her neck, and a bunch of holly at her breast, and as her walked up the room with her head held high, and her eyes a-shining like two stars, she looked like a queen for sure, and so thought more than one.

Mother was standing close behind the two squires when Malvina she first came in sight. She saw the old man start and catch hold to the arms of his chair, while the young master just took a step back, and saith quick in her ear,

'Who the devil is that girl, Thirza? What a beauty! Where on earth have you hidden her? Why she steps like a queen! Jove! what a beauty!'

'Her be Malvina,' mother saith quiet, 'and her lives out to Witches' Combe.'

'Good Lord!' he saith, 'and I've seen many a duchess who'd have given every diamond she possessed to walk through a room like that. What a perfect head? Thirza woman, I can't make it out.'

And he never took his eyes off her from that moment, no more did the old Squire.

As ill luck would have it, Jan got Malvina into the crosshand dance just alongside of Joan Richards. He see'd a bit of a gap and took her right in never noticing who was next to him, though he'd have given his eyes to have changed it the moment he saw how it was.

Malvina in passing touched Joan's arm, and Joan she turned in a moment and saw who was next. Her face grew crimson with rage, and her flinged right out of the dance altogether.

'I b'aint going to stand next the Witch's Maid!' her said, tossing her head, 'not very likely!'

She spoke out shrill and clear so as all the room heard her, and the folks stopped dancing, and Jimmy Crick a-fiddling. 'How dare such a one come along with us?' screamed Joan, stamping her foot. She was fairly beside herself with rage, seeing who 'twas had brought Malvina into the dance, and she didn't care what she said. For Joan had a terrible tongue, and knew how to use it, and when she was in one of her rages, no person could stop her.

The folk had all drawn away from Malvina, and every eye in the room was on the maid. Maybe there was a man or two among them who would have liked to have said a word for her, only Joan's tongue was too much for them. As for the women folk, well some was really feared of her, and the rest thought it best to leave her alone, and were curious to see what would happen. Jan he came over and took Malvina's hand, and then Joan went properly mad.

'You daring witch!' she saith, 'a-coming along of respectable folk. Who knows what they may wake up with to-morrow, spotted faces and all sorts? Ah! you wicked, daring thing; go back to Witches' Combe and bide there, for you won't find as decent folk will have anything to do with ye. Look to Jan Williams there!' she cried with a shrill laugh, pointing with her finger, while her face just flamed with passion, 'witched, if ever a man was witched, so as he can't help following her wherever she goes whether he likes it or no. You'd best look out,' her saith with a sneering laugh to the other maids, ''twill be your turn soon, and not a maid to Withyford will be able to keep her man.' Malvina took her hand from Jan's and moved a step away from him, and seeing she wished it, so he let her be; though his heart was just yearning to fight them all for her sake.

So the maid stood by herself, quiet and tall, holding her head like a queen's, while a red spot burned on either cheek, and she caught her lip tight between her snowy teeth.

When Joan had fairly given in because she'd no more breath; Malvina her just looked round to all the folk as if she'd strip their very souls; and more than one shrank back from her as her clear eye flashed. And then she spoke, and every word her saith came out as clear as a bell.

'You need not be afeard, any of you,' her saith; 'for I be going. But afore I do go, I ask you plain all in this here room, have. I ever done ought to harm any man, woman, or child to Withyford Town? They lie who say I have and you know it! You be cowards all, and I scorn you as the dirt under my feet. Touch you?' she cried, while her sweet lips trembled, 'dance with you? mix with you? no, never again, you need not be afeard, I be going!'

And she turned quickly round, her eyes bright with anger, her lips all to a quiver, and walked swiftly down the room towards the door.

But afore she got there, the young Squire was alongside of her. 'Please stay one moment,' he saith, 'for I want you to dance with me, that is to say if you will, Malvina; strike up Jimmy!' And afore Malvina knew where she was, her was up the middle and down again, with the young Squire's arm about her waist, and his strong young hand in hers. And you may be sure as there weren't one in the room as dare question the young Squire's partner.

The moment as Jimmy Crick had stopped the dance through giving in with his fiddle, Malvina, she slipped from the Squire's arms, afore he knew, and was out of the door, and into the kitchen to mother. Her breath was coming quick, mother saith, and her eyes shone like two stars, and her cheeks were glowing as roses fresh picked.

'I must be going,' her saith. 'Goodbye Thirza!',and she unhung her cloak from the door and began aputting of it on.

'You surely b'aint going yet awhile?' mother saith, 'why, the folks haven't had supper yet, and how can I get along with only Liz? I can't get on without ye, my dear!'

'But you *must*, Thirza,' her saith quick and sharp. 'Now don't go and stop me, there's a dear soul! I b'aint going to face one of they folk again to-night, no, never again if I can help it. For I've been shamed afore the whole of Withyford, and I'm going to give no person the chance of doing it again. I was foolish even to put foot inside these doors, to-night be the last time I've a-done it.'

Malvina's hands were trembling, so as she scarce could tie up her hood. The tears were standing on her lashes, but her face kept proud and haughty for all that. Mother saw as it weren't a bit of use to try and turn her from her purpose, so she just let her be, and said nought. But she felt a bit sore to think as Malvina should speak so, for 'twas only for the maiden's good that she'd brought her at all to Grange.

Sudden, as if Malvina guessed what mother was thinking, she kissed her quick and got her lovely arms about her.

'Now don't you, don't you, Thirza,' her saith, 'go and think ought against me. You be the only person in the world who cares a scat about me, and that I know. I b'aint ungrateful, and you mustn't think it, but I can't come to Grange again. I can't, I can't!'

'There, there,' saith mother, 'don't take on so, dear maid. There be other folk as love ye, without old Thirza. Oh yes there be, and time will make mention who?'

'Hush!' Malvina said, 'there be someone coming!' and afore mother could stop her, she was out of the door and round to the back, and in another minute she heard her quick feet pass the window, and the crisp frost crackling under her tread.

Winter on an Exmoor Farm

ALICE R. ELLIOTT, 1970

Low lies the farmstead by the hill
Safe from the wild beyond,
The swirling mist floats damp and chill,
December keeps her bond.
Across the heather, aged and spent,
An early darkness creeps,
The ghosts of trees gaunt, gnarled and bent,
Rise from the rocky steeps.

Warm and safe from the brooding moor
The beasts lie in the byre,
My lighted lantern at the door
Glows with a warmer fire;
For as I pause awhile with them
And in their musing share,
I link that byre with Bethlehem
And see a baby there.

Christmas at the Vicarage

From *Wanderings in Devon*, 1887

J.M. CHANTER

Christmas at the vicarage was a time of joyful expectation to all, being of greater importance because Mrs Chanter's Birthday fell on Christmas Eve. In old days there were no lack of 'Waits' in Ilfracombe, and long before Christmas they met togther to practise the fine old anthems and carols, which had been handed down from father to son for generations. There were the Prices, Germans, Challacombes, and Conibears, all had been 'singing families' for generations; and there was old Galliver with his bass viol, to lead them. One party of 'Waits' always sang outside the dining-room windows on Christmas Eve while the family were at dinner; to them the children carried oranges and other dainties. But the party who came in the middle of the night were by far the most exciting in the children's eyes, for it necessitated being huddled out of bed into shawls and other wraps, and to be sat in the deep window-sills of the rooms overlooking the drive. There peeping from behind the blinds, they could see the dusky forms below, by the light of their horn lanterns, and how their faces used to glow. Then after much scuffling, clearing of throats and conversational mumblings, would come the exciting tum, tum, tum, from Galliver's bass viol. A voice would then say on one note, with great rapidity 'While Shepherds watched their flocks by night,' then they would start launching forth into marvellous intricacies of song. Here a treble voice would take the solo, clear and strong, then a tenor with many turns and quavers, then the whole body would join in with a real burst of harmony. ('Crown Him Lord of All' was a special favourite of Mrs Chanters, it is a beautiful tune, and a thousand pities it should be lost.) After they had sung two or three carols, they would adjourn to the kitchen for refreshment, where annual jokes were cracked, and the mistletoe was discussed. So the children would scamper back to bed, with one eye open to keep watch for *Santa Claus*, while the maids hurried downstairs to help their mistress entertain the carollers. That night all the little bedposts were hung with stockings to receive the gifts of *Santa Claus*, who never failed to fill them.

Exmoor Carols

From *Carols of the Westcountry*, 1996

GLYN COURT

Glyn Court has done the musical heritage of the Westcountry an immeasurable service by collecting the local carols that sprang largely from the region's West Gallery (that is, the Church Band before the coming of the now ubiquitous organ) tradition. Their music, as he says, possessed 'singable melodies to simple words, the full throatedness of the open air and the living pulse of the dance.' Here, by way of introduction to four Exmoor carols, he discusses one of the leading practitioners of the art, Thomas Slade, the Roadwater blacksmith.

Tom had been born in the late 1830s as one of the ten children of John Slade, who earned a precarious living by cracking stones by the wayside for a shilling a day. It was drudgery and back-breaking toil, but one day a Bible Christian travelling preacher stopped to speak to him and found the words to awaken an unsuspected emotion in his heart and raise his eyes from the dead end of stonecracking to the hills of hope. His affairs began to prosper and he was able to apprentice Tom to the village blacksmith. In the Slades there was a strong vein of music and both Tom and his brother William conceived the desire of learning the instrument which formed the backbone of a church orchestra: the 'cello or bass viola. Tom put together enough from his meagre earnings, set off early one morning and walked the 20 hilly miles to Taunton, bought the 'cello, strapped it on his back and walked the 20 miles home with it the same afternoon – and still put in two or three hours in the forge before retiring to bed.

It is not clear whether the band had expired and Tom revived it, but certainly under him the old tradition of the 'waits' prospered, and continued long after it had lapsed elsewhere. He was not a humourless man, but his upbringing had given him a vein of sternness and he was something of a disciplinarian with his musicians. As Christmas approached he rehearsed them, and year after year on Christmas Eve, when the village had retired to rest, a little before midnight the musicians came with their instruments into the warm 'pentice' of Tom's smithy, and he would invite them into his parlour for cordials and cakes to give them courage for the long, cold round. Then they set off in a happy group for their first call, an Elizabethan farmhouse half a mile up the valley. Talk and slow laughter went to and fro. But as they drew near the farm Tom would issue his first command and they would fall silent. He knew how precious a part of great music is silence, but beyond that, as a man of deep emotion, he felt that while speech was man's distinctive attribute, music was divine, and the sleepers must be awakened not by idle chatter but by a noble harmony, a 'concord of sweet sounds'. So they gathered by the door, Thomas counted four beats, the instruments sounded the great G major chord, and in measured, stentorian tones he announced the first carol:

Mortals – awake! Rejoice – and sing

The glories – of – your heav'nly – King!

The notes rang out and presently a candle glimmered in an upstairs window, and as the carol ended the door opened and the farmer's wife invited them in for hot refreshment. Then they would go to the next farm and repeat the performance, and so move on through the starry silence till about three o'clock in the morning, when they returned to the bridge in the middle of the village to play in the holy day with:-

Once more, behold! The day is come,

The bright and glorious morn!

Let every tongue on earth rejoice

For Christ the Lord is born –

'and what more entrancing,' wrote Lewis Court, who heard it every year as a boy, 'than to be awakened by the strains of Christmas music stealing in upon one through the silence of the night, or on the clean air of a frosty morning! – the deep, full tones of the bass viol, the celestial notes of the clarinet, the suave, appealing plaint of the flute, and the blend of good human voices.' Half a lifetime later he could 'never think of the Bethlehem story of the angels' song without its association with those rare old carols, with their fantastic runs and their sweet, simple harmonies, that once a year made musical the haunts of ancient peace' in his beloved vale.

MORTALS, AWAKE! REJOICE AND SING

Roadwater, Somerset

1 Mortals, awake! Rejoice and sing
The glories of your heav'nly King

REFRAIN
Rejoice in hope, rejoice with me,
Ye shall from all your sins be free

2 Come, let us all our voices raise
And loudly sound with songs of praise

3 Let all in heav'n and all on earth
Rejoice in their Redeemer's birth

AWAKE, YOUR GRATEFUL VOICES RAISE

Roadwater, Leighland, and Exford, Somerset

1: Verse 2: C-tenor / Treble and Alto complete "mortals" on C; verse 4, similarly for

1 Awake, your grateful voices raise!
In this great cause let all conspire:
How could we sing our Saviour's praise
In strains like the celestial choir.

2 They celebrated Jesus Christ
With hymns of harmony divine:
So with us mortals here on earth
In one great choir let all combine.

3 And may our God grant us His peace
And make us of one heart and mind,
And may we all through Jesus Christ
His mercy and forgiveness find.

4 All glory be to God on high,
Who sits enthroned above the skies;
The great, the mighty Lord adore,
Who lives both now and evermore.

CHRISTIANS, AWAKE! AWAKE AND SING!

Porlock, Somerset

Christ- ians, a- wake! a- wake and sing *p* The birth of Christ our Lord *§* The birth of Christ our Lord: He hath ap- peared on earth as King Ac- cord- ing to His word *§* Ac- cord- ing to His word He hath ap- peared He hath ap- peared on earth as King Ac- cord- ing to His word

1 Christians, awake! awake and sing
The birth of Christ our Lord.
He hath appeared on earth as King,
According to His word.

2 On Bethl'em's plains a sound was heard
That ne'er was heard before:
To you a King is born, and He
Shall reign for evermore.

3 It was the choir of heaven that sang
The great Redeemer's birth:
Glory to God, good-will to man
And lasting peace on earth.

4 We too would now renew the theme
And all our voices raise
To Christ the Babe of Bethlehem,
The King of endless days.

I HEAR ALONG OUR STREET

Arr. G. C.   Dunster.

I hear a-long our street — Pass the min-strel throngs: Hark! they play so

sweet on their haut-boys, Christ-mas songs **Refrain** Let us by the fire ev- er

higher, ev- er higher Sing un- til the night ex- pire Sing un- til the night ex- pire

1 I hear along our street
Pass the minstrel throngs.
Hark! they play so sweet
On their hautboys Christmas songs.

2 In December ring
Every day the chimes;
Loud the gleemen sing
In the street their merry rhymes.

3 Shepherds at the grange
Where the Child was born,
Sang, with many a change,
Christmas carols until morn

4 Who by the fireside stands
Stamps his feet and sings,
But he who blows his hands
Not so gay a carol brings.

REFRAIN
Let us by the fire
Ever higher, ever higher,
Sing until the night expire,
Sing until the night expire.

Christmas! Christmas!

From *The Linhay on the Downs*, 1929

H. WILLIAMSON

Henry Williamson was born in a London suburb, but settled in Devon after the First World War, and since then has been associated indelibly with the county. In 1929, with his wife Loetitia and young family, he moved to Shallowford, at Filleigh, on the southern flank of Exmoor.

Why should not this Christmas be the best one has known? The children are beginning to be human beings, with their own personalities, and therefore as companions they are stimulating. Also, we are looking forward as eagerly to our guests' coming as, we hope, they are eagerly anticipating their arrival. It had been fun arranging the bedrooms, and finding odd corners for camp beds.

And the walks we shall have, whatever the weather, on the high ground of Exmoor and in the lanes, with their tall beechen hedges! The blazing of wood fires on open hearths shall greet us when we return, pleasantly tired, to sip tea made from the black iron kettle hanging on its lapping crook from the chimney bar.

I have got a spruce fir, with all its roots; it is set in an oak tub, for later planting-out in the hilltop field. The sapling shall not be murdered; it shall, after Christmas, join the company of its brethren below Windwhistle Spinney. Late on Christmas Eve, when the children are lying excitedly awake upstairs, or breathing sweetly in sleep, we and our friends will deck its branches with shimmering delights. Then into the cupboard under the stairs, until the afternoon party.

Of course everyone will hang out a stocking. And of course Father Christmas will fill each stocking, and everyone will sit at the long refectory table for breakfast. On one side the children, graded according to size, from the gipsy-dark Margaret to the speedwell-eyed Ann – on the other ourselves, the so-called adults, watching happy faces over the table.

Afterwards a two-mile walk across park and fields to church. On the way we shall peer over the parapet of the bridge to see if any of the spawning salmon are visible.

Before the church service everyone greets everyone else in voices that are neither loud nor yet subdued. Contrast is the salt of life; and, after the singing of the good old hymns, we shall return in an amazingly short time to see the turkey turning slowly on the jack-spit by the hearth. And what a fire! The wood for it has been selected and matured for several years. Pine, for the resinous scents; oak for body; elm for its majestic white ash; alder for its charcoal – the flames of these woods will blend and be thrown out by the bulk of the yew-wood back-brand.

The twin rows of human cormorants will perch themselves along our table, I shall refuse to carve, corks will pop with bubble of grape and ginger; the lighted pudding, set with holly sprigs, will come in, with the mince pies, to be eyed with lessening enthusiasm except by the rows of brighter

Wartime Christmas Party at the Lion Hotel, Dulverton. 1941.

faces. Who will want figs, dates or nuts? Then for the crackers.

There will be ping-pong, skittles, bagatelle, lead-horse racing, crown-and-anchor, and maybe (since Harold is of the party) the three card trick. And those of us who have realized the poise and harmony between life and death will meet in my writing-room, to listen and to think as the voice of the King, symbol of our hopes for our brother men and neighbours, speaks around the earth.

Yes: this Christmas, I hope, will be proper. Windles, the eldest boy, has just come in to tell me he has seen Father Christmas's reindeer! They were going up the path to Bremridge Wood … or else they were the red deer from Exmoor, driven down by the hard weather. Which were they, Dad?

Quick Windles, tell the others what you've seen! Christmas! Christmas!

Exmoor Nativity

BERTA LAWRENCE, 1980

Bright star ahead of him over Dunkery
The only light tonight.
Moon is swallowed, lesser stars in flight
Beyond the scudding wrack of cloud.
The roof of the moor is black,
But this is the right way home.
Bare feet know the pattern of pebbles
Paving the track, the contour of moss-mats,
The surface of slabs overlying a stream.

Now the path has topped the slope.
He sees the warm glow-worm light of home
And starts to trot as the track falls down.
A dead hare swings from his belt,
Taken in his withy-snare on the marsh.
His arrow has brought down a wild duck,
A handful of pebbles jingle in his pouch,
Picked up on the shore to please a woman.

His wattle hut dim with smoky reek,
Clay saucer of oil with simmering wick,
An old woman babbling glad tidings
And his own woman on their bed of skins,
Holding, wrapped in lambskin,
A wailing child, newborn and blood-streaked.

Beyond seas and mountains
Another child is born
Inside a cave-stable
Under a star.

Christmas Day

From *Living on Exmoor,* 1963

HOPE BOURNE

A dawn wind, like a benediction, sweet and strong, bringing all the scent of the moor and the sea over the hedges and into the fields. A little early sunshine and patches of blue sky looking through the moving sou'west clouds, and the sheep lying in a garland across the big field, just raising their heads at the sound of footsteps in the morning light. A moorland Christmas – Christmas Day in the morning.

From out of space the strains of *Adeste Fideles* come clear on the wind, coming from a distant wireless set by an open door, and the sheep themselves seem like a Christmas carol as they look up from the grass. Robins trill from the hedges as I pass and cows low from the shippons in the yard, and somewhere a cock crows to add his voice to the sounds of early morning. A green Christmas, and we are glad to see it.

Away over the fields the little moorland church beyond the hill waits for its worshippers from afar. Soon its bells will ring, and its folk will come, a few on foot, but most in cars and Land-rovers, for the hill country parish is wide and scattered. I think of it now, and remember its small squat tower of rough grey stone, with the ferns that have come to roost in the crannies, inside as well as out, green fingers above the bell-ropes. I remember the narrow nave, and the chancel decked with holly, and the steps down from the door with the big wide view of the heather-dark moor and the woods in the valley below. Little grey church – it has sat a long time on its hillside in the sun and the wind since first its stones were raised, and forgotten hands set the round Norman arch above the open door. Last night it was lit with lamps and candles; this morning the sun shines through its coloured glass and soon there will be singing again under the timbered roof. Once more men will come to listen to a story told again and again, and to remember in their hearts an older rejoicing in the triumph of light over darkness.

Christmas Day on a hill farm differs not in any material way from any other day, save that a few folk may try to get down to the church for the morning service. The beasts must be fed and tended and the sheep looked to as usual, and all the heavy yard work done and all the

E.R.J. Davey

Withypool.

innumerable odd chores accomplished. The midday meal is usually a scratch one, for the Christmas dinner is put back to the evening so that all can eat in peace after the last of the day's tasks are done and the beasts bedded down for the night.

The days of Christmas are short and the nights long, but they are seldom really cold. One does not look for snow and hard weather until after New Year. December is usually an open month and a green Christmas the rule. Only once do I remember a white Christmas when it snowed in the morning and turned to a blizzard in the afternoon, and the cattle came back into the shippons covered with white like the ornaments on a Christmas cake. But snow, despite its beauty and though it may represent the traditional image of Christmas, is a thing no one desires to see in the hills until one must. It is the green winter that is always hoped for, despite its disadvantages.

So the day's work goes on until it is time again to see to the sheep. Dusk comes quickly on the heels of the short afternoon, and I take my staff and step out quickly for the top fields. Westward, the last rays of the setting sun pierce the cloud in glory like the light from an altar. In the flaming light I lift my eyes and look up at the five great hills that raise their heads all around, barrow-crowned every one. Many are the nameless ones whose spirits must brood over the heights where once in life they hunted and fought and lusted, and where now their ashes sleep in the earth. This night we keep their festival and ours, the turning of the year, the rising of the sun, the step from darkness into light, life and hope and the promise of all things made new. Strange that the Christian birth should be one with the ancient festival of resurgent life. Or perhaps not so strange.

And now it is dusk, and all the beasts are fed and settled for the night, the sheep in the field, the cows in the shippon, the horses in the stable. The lights glow in the house, there is bustle in the kitchen, an undercurrent of anticipation – and at last we sit down to our long-awaited dinner. A mighty feast it is, with a turkey so big that it will hardly go on the largest dish for the centre-piece, and so many things else that we can barely consume them all. A merry Christmas to us all, and many more to come!

Late at night I rise from the fire, and take a turn around the yard, and with lantern in hand look into those buildings where beasts are tied, making sure all is well. The light throws monstrous shadows from the dozing beasts on to the rough walls behind. In the last shippon, that next to the stable, a huge figure stands against the wall, almost touching the low ceiling. It is our great red bull, and as he turns his ponderous head, sleepy-eyed, the light catches at his thick white horns. Beside him two cows lie at rest, and by his head a small calf sleeps. The light and shadow moulds them, making of them a sculptured group, and they seem without time, as though they had always been like that. They are figures from a manger scene, living counterparts of those small images set forth in wood last night within the crib in the bright lamp-lit church. A happy Christmas to you, beasts in the straw, for perhaps you know more than we do on this Christmas night.

Christmas Recipes

BRIAN PEARCE

Over the last few years, Brian Pearce (with Heather Burnett-Wells) has been rediscovering the distinctive cookery of Exmoor in a series of articles for Exmoor – The Country Magazine *and the* Magnum Opus Exmoor Food and Cookery. *In a 1998 piece for the magazine, Brian explained the context of Christmas food on Exmoor and ventured some traditional recipes for a seasonal feast.*

The sort of Christmas we are all used to, with Santa, cards, presents, Christmas trees, turkey and Christmas pudding, was unknown on Exmoor before Victorian times. Such festivities were really a nineteenth century way for the middle classes to keep up with the Joneses, the Joneses in this case being the Royal Family. Until then feasting was mostly the prerogative of the wealthy. If ordinary people feasted it was usually at the invitation of a wealthy landlord or employer.

Traditional at Christmas Eve on Exmoor is the ashen faggot custom. The faggot is a bundle of ash sticks tied with thin green wands of ash, willow, hazel or beech. The number of ties varies from household to household and has much to do with the size of the faggot, which in turn is determined by the size of the fireplace. The faggot is placed on the fire and as the ties burn through they tend to snap. As each snaps it is toasted with mulled ale or cider and toast made against the fire. Guests were greeted with spiced bread or wigs, rather like the mince pies of today. The ceremony is a version of wassailing which simply means wishing good health for the coming year. The practice clearly has roots in pagan fertility rites and is applied to crops as well as humans, and apple crops in particular. The apple was an important feature of Christmas and New Year festivities. If the sun shone through the branches of the apple tree on Christmas morning or if the branches were covered with snow it portended a good crop in the following season.

On Christmas morning farm and estate labourers were invited 'up to the house' with their wives and offered spiced ale and cider. Farmers would often invite their labourers with their families to dinner. From Tudor times onwards goose was the traditional fare. Lonely farms have always been difficult to police and many Exmoor farms had a goose house, rather like a kennel, near the back door for a gander to warn of strangers approaching. Goose was also the dish at Michaelmas (29 September), the end of a year's service for labourers and the time when tenants paid their rents. This was another occasion when such people would be invited up to the house and goose was traditional for this occasion too as geese were fattened on the gleanings from the corn harvest.

CHRISTMAS GOOSE

Roast goose was traditionally stuffed with prunes and apples and served with apple, bread or gooseberry sauce. In other areas the fruit stuffing was turned into sauce with the addition of wine. As it was a luxury dish and there is little meat on it for its size, the goose was commonly stuffed with rabbit joints to give to the children whilst the adults feasted on the poultry.

1 goose
juice of ¹/₂ lemon
butter
seasoning

FOR THE STUFFING
8 oz breadcrumbs
2 cooking apples
2 oz prunes
1 teaspoon sage
1 onion
1 oz butter
seasoning

Remove any accessible fat from the goose. Weigh the goose. Rub with lemon juice and season. Peel, core and dice the apple. Soak and stone the prunes if necessary and chop. Mix all the stuffing ingredients together, binding with the melted butter. Place the stuffing in the cavity of the goose. Put the goose in a roasting dish and dot with butter. Cover and roast in the oven at 350°F/180°C/Gas Mark 4 for twenty minutes per pound and an extra twenty minutes. Take the lid off for the last thirty minutes of cooking. The goose can be served with gravy made with stock from the giblets, if any, and the cooking juices from which the fat has been drained.

NORTH DEVON BLACK CAKE

The term black cake seems to refer to many dark fruit cakes. I use this as my Christmas cake recipe, although it is a cake for any festive celebration. It is not cheap to make and is definitely one for special occasions. It matures well and the tradition is to bake two and keep one for the anniversary of the occasion for which the cake was baked. You can, of course, halve the quantities and only bake one if you wish. The Cornish variation of this cake omits the treacle, so it is not as moist and, therefore, not so much like a Christmas pudding after a year.

½ lb plain flour
½ lb rice flour
12 eggs
¾ lb butter
½ lb caster sugar
6 oz treacle
4 lb mixed fruit and peel
½ lb chopped almonds
2 tablespoons brandy or rum
2 teaspoons baking powder
4 teaspoons ground mixed spice

Whisk the eggs in a bain marie or a basin over a large bowl of hot water until they are light and creamy. Cream together the butter and sugar and gradually add the eggs and warmed treacle. Gradually fold in the sieved flours, baking powder and spices. Mix in the fruit, nuts and spirits. Divide the mixture between two lined and greased 9-inch cake tins. Bake at 350°F/ 180°C/Gas Mark 4 for three hours. Turn out the cakes when cool. It is best to leave them for at least a week before using, preferably longer. They are usually covered with marzipan and iced a few days before use. Don't do this to the one you want to keep until just before it is needed, or you will end up with a brown sticky mess.

FRUMENTY OR PLUM PORRIDGE

This dish developed as a simple porridge in medieval times, made into a broth with meat bones. It was later sweetened with honey and then fruit and wine were added for special occasions. The fruit included prunes, which gave rise to the term plum pudding. Eventually the meat disappeared, the fruit became the dominant ingredient and the frumenty developed into Christmas pudding which as we know it was made popular by Prince Albert in the nineteenth century. The recipe for this pudding dates from the early eighteenth century and was prepared for George I, who was known as the Pudding King. It is similar to today's Christmas pudding but there is a high proportion of prunes in the fruit, which is bound with a large number of eggs.

Frumenty, which was once widespread, remained a tradition in Somerset. You can try the original variety by adding to a simmering beef broth dried fruit, spices and a fruit liqueur with a thickener of breadcrumbs or semolina to make a porridge. The later form is like a hot muesli. The following is an old recipe using fresh wheat with the husks removed. Pearl barley can be substituted.

10 oz wheat

1¹/₂ pt water

2 pt milk

4 oz dried fruit: currants, raisins, sultanas or prunes

2 egg yolks

grated rind of 1 lemon

sugar and spice to taste

Wash the wheat and cover with water in an earthenware jar or bowl. Stand in a warm place for at least a day – the top of a Rayburn is ideal. The wheat will absorb the water and make a gelatinous gruel called creed wheat. Boil the creed wheat in the milk and when it begins to thicken add the sugar, spice, fruit and lemon rind. Finally stir in the egg yolks to thicken the mixture further.

WASSAIL CUP

Modern Exmoor wassail cups tend to be mulled cider, especially when part of the wassailing of apple trees. Beer, however, was more commonly used, especially on Christmas Eve.

There are no detailed recipes for wassail cups as ingredients were, as now, generally added to taste and never repeated exactly. A simple method was to heat ale slowly in a pan, without boiling, and add sliced apples, cloves, nutmeg, cinnamon and sugar. In some recipes the beer was refermented by adding yeast and sugar. Spices were added and it was allowed to brew for a few days before straining into a wassail bowl with hot roasted apples and sherry or some other fortification.

WIGS

Wigs were used as sops to dip in the mulled ale, cider or wassail cup. The name is thought to come from wigge, the old word for wedge, as these yeast cakes were made like a bun round to be divided into wedge-shaped sections. Cut with a cross, they are a reminder of other festive cakes such as hot cross and revel buns.

I like this recipe as my yeast buns have a habit of rising sideways rather than outwards and in this case that is what they are supposed to do. Also I tend to get as much dough on myself as in the mixing bowl and the large amount of fat in this mixture means that it does not stick like bread dough. On Exmoor clotted cream would almost certainly have replaced the butter and cream in this old recipe, which I have adapted for the use of modern easy-cook dried yeast.

INGREDIENTS FOR 7–9 WIGS
1 lb plain flour
2 teaspoons salt
$^1/_2$ oz dried yeast
$^1/_2$ lb butter
2$^1/_2$ fluid oz single cream
$^1/_2$ teaspoon each of ground nutmeg, mace and cloves
1 egg
1 oz caraway seeds
4 oz caster sugar
sugar and water to glaze

Sift the flour into a basin with the salt and spices and mix in the quick dried yeast according to the manufacturer's instructions. Melt together the butter and cream and beat in the egg. Pour all into a well in the centre of the flour, mix well and knead lightly. Leave in the bowl to rest for a few minutes. Knead in the sugar and caraway seeds. Roll the dough out thinly. The cakes used to be baked on earthenware saucers or small plates. I cut round a saucer to obtain the shape and place them on greased baking trays. Score each deeply with a knife to form a cross and leave in a warm place to prove – about an hour. Bake at 425°F/220°C/Gas Mark 7 for ten to fifteen minutes until golden brown. Brush with a sugar and water glaze whilst still warm.

The Old Fashion Devonshire Gammon Pie –
A Christmas Cornucopia

An old recipe from just beyond Exmoor's southern fringes.

The Writer, Henry Parker, once of Loosedon Barton, Winkleigh, North Devon, well remembers the labour and trouble his (late) Mother used to take in making one of these pies every Christmas. This huge pie would consist of the following.

One large ham, the largest the farm would provide during the year, three or four couple of chicken jointed, ox tongues etc.

She used to make a large quantity of dough, the bottom, sides, and cover, all composed of dough. The ham would be placed in the centre, chicken and tongues round it. It was made on a very wide plank or two planks fastened together. When ready and the huge oven sufficiently heated, it would take two powerful men, usually Rd Knight (still living aged eighty-nine) and Simon Down, labourers, to place it into the oven, when baked it would be placed in the Hall. It was usually tapped by Christmas waits, on Christmas eve or morning, as the case might be. These were The Parish Church Choir, Leader, the late Mr Arthur Friend, Henry Keenor, who is still living, and others, with good voices and string instruments the best Choir then in North Devon. They would go around to the farm houses singing Christmas carols and generally did not arrive at Loosedon Barton until the small hours of Christmas morning, they usually sang a couple of carols under the windows when one of them with a loud voice would wish the people a good evening or morning as the case might be. Mr and Mrs so and so we wish you a Merry Christmas and a Happy New Year, you and all your good family. They would then be called in the house and partake of the Gammon Pie, after that the pie was kept on the bale in the Hall, and any and every person calling during the Christmas (and callers were numerous) were invited to help themselves, I recollect too that we boys (several of us), used to get a peer share, it was for the visitors and callers, and every one were welcome, to eat, and drink as much nut brown ale and cider as they choosed. These were happy days, and old fashioned Christmas. Alas these are all passed away.

Henry Parker, Watchet.   Bridgewater, 17/11/1898

Exmoor at Christmas

MAUREEN HOSEGOOD, 1967

Stars bang on red-dropped holly boughs,
And shine like tears upon the mistletoe,
And great logs burn, and candles nod and gleam
Like waxen flowers on satin, pearl-spiked leaves.

An almost bridal purity persists:
A fierce, white flame of longing, unfulfilled;
And then the bells have ceased, and folk return
Shaking their coats, and calling their goodnights
And bolting doors...

Out in the woods the snow lies quiet,
And on the hillsides there are shepherds still,
And in men's hearts are images of peace.
Caractacus would have wondered at the bells.
The old, dark legend of the mistletoe
Was all he knew. His stone was old and worn
Before the Christ was born.

The bells have rung, the carols have been sung
In every vale and combe,
But up on Winsford Hill the cruel wind
Buffets the heather. By the ancient way
The stone
Stands silent and alone.

The Old Minehead Christmas Mummers' Play

To shorten winters' sadness,
See where the folks with gladness
Disguised all are coming
Right wantonly a-mumming.

Mummers plays were a sure part of the Christmas scene until the days of Queen Victoria. The plays are thought to date form the early Middle Ages and are found – with variations – in many parts of the country. Usually they are based on the story of St George fighting with a Turkish Knight: Christianity overcoming paganism, and therefore particularly suitable for Christmas. Over the centuries other more topical references and characters (particularly around the time of the Napoleonic Wars) were added along with a knock-about figure or two to make the whole thing more like a pantomime. The local cast would travel from place to place over the Christmas period, working to a 'script' that was generally not written down but which descended from generation to generation by word of mouth; consequently each play was particular to its own locality. As the mummers began to die out in the nineteenth century, efforts were made to capture the texts before they were lost irretrievably. The Minehead Mummers' Play *was revived at Christmas in 1908 by the members of the Guild of St George, and subsequently published in a version by Clement Kille.*

CHARACTERS.

First Mummer	Admiral Duncan
Second Mummer	Lord Nelson
Old Father Christmas	General Wolfe
Dame Dorrity	Giant Beelzebub
St. George	Slasher, the Valiant Man
Valentine, the Morocco King.	Little Man Jan
Prince Imbridge	Tom Bowling
Sambo	King John
Doctor	Queen Susan
Turkish Knight	

NOTES.

The words of the old Minehead Mummers' Play were taken down from Mr. John Thorne, of Alcombe, a Minehead Mummer of long ago. They have been closely followed here, but in a few places unsuitable words and apparently meaningless sentences have been altered, and new lines have occasionally been added, for the purpose, in some measure, of linking together the various parts. The parts of Father Christmas and Dame Dorrity, who are the buffoons of the piece, depended a great deal on the impromptu wit of the performers, and the dialogue here has been slightly extended towards the end of the piece. Several characters have had to be omitted, their lines being practically the same as those of others in the play. Mummers in different parts of the country seem to have added characters according to local fancy, and in the Minehead play there were nearly thirty. The assumption of another character was a very simple matter, one of the performers merely going off and returning under another name, with little or no change of costume. The parts of King John and Queen Susan were apparently introduced from some other traditional play, and also the finishing song. In an old sword-dancing play, a favourite at one time in the North of England, the principal characters were called on for the dance with a song of very similar words. The short dialogue after Tom Bowling's speech is not in the original. It has been added to lead up to the entrance of King John and Queen Susan.

C. KILLE, Avalon, Minehead,

The Minehead Mummers' Play.

Scene: A BARONIAL HALL.

Voices outside: Open thy doors.

Curtain rises.

Enter Two Mummers. They salute.

First Mummer: Gentlemen, ladies, upon my forehead!
It's on my shoulder I carry my sword,
I show my sport, I bend my rhyme,
And now I'm fit for Christmas time.
'Tis now in the merry time of Christmas,
And Christmas draweth near,
I hope your pockets are full of money
And your cellars full of beer.
And if you believe not what I say,
Walk in, Old Father Christmas, and boldly
    clear the way. *(They retire, R).*

Enter Father Christmas, L.

Father: Here comes I, Old Father Christmas;
Welcome or welcome not,
I hope Old Father Christmas
Will never be forgot.
When, in the midst of summer,
The sun it shineth hot,
'Tis then Old Father Christmas
Is almost quite forgot.
But now, in the winter time,
When his old grey beard is frozen with ice,
And his old bald head is covered with snow,
I hope you'll make him welcome before I go.

(Marches round).

Enter Dame Dorrity L.

Dame: Here comes I, old Mother Dorrity,
Fat face and go marity;
Head big and body small,
The purtiest little cratur' amongst us all.

4

Father : What say? the purtiest little woman amongst us
all?
The ugliest old jade amongst us all.
Can't I never go out to a ladies' and gentlemen's
party,
But thee art always larripin' after me?

Dame :—Thee out to a ladies' and gentlemen's party!
All thee dost mind is after the ladies.

Father : And all thee dost mind is after the fellows! So
there's a pair of us. What dost want me home for?
(*beats her*).

Dame : Come home to supper (*beats him*).

Father : What's got for supper?

Dame : A good old favourite of thine.

Father : What's got?

Dame : A girt dish of water porridge.

Father : A girt dish of water porridge and a girt long
pitching-pick to ate it wi'!
Porridge so thin. I do suppose,
I'll have to doff all my small clothes,
And jump in round to catch the bread.

Dame (*beats him*) : That's good enough for thee, thee old rogue

Father : What's got for theeself?

Dame : Tea, toast, and butter ; tea, toast, and butter.

Father : Tea, toast, and butter! Anything is good enough for
me!
I tell thee what, old woman,
I'll tell thee a little of thy own.

Dame : What can'st thee tell me?

Father (*leaning forward on his stick*) :
Dost mind the time when thee was up in Jossy
Hosegood's fuzzy-brake?
When the wind blowed high,
And the wind blowed low ;
And the wind blowed puff——

Dame (*knocks away his stick, and he falls*) :
And down thee didst go.

Father (*rising*) : Sudden change this, from my last wife,
When I had a silver watch in my pocket and
a gold guard hanging out.
Now I'm walking about with my trousers a-
broke, and my sleeves hanging out.

Dame (*beating him round*) : Good enough for thee, thee old
rogue.

5

Father: Ah! I tell thee what, old woman!
If thee dissn't mind my words
Thee shan't be my blowse.
So thee hook it (*drives her out, L*).

Father (*laughing*): I've driven the old jade out at last.
Although I'm come, I have short time to stay;
Then, walk in, St. George, and boldly clear the way.
Enter, brave Champion, and boldly act thy part,
And let the noble company see thou hast a lion's
heart. (*Exit Father Christmas, L*).

Enter St. George, R.

St. George: Here come I, St. George, I've many hazards
run,
And fought in every land that lies beneath
the sun.
I am a famous champion,
Likewise a worthy knight,
And from old Britain did I spring
And will uphold her might.
I travelled countries far and near,
As you may understand,
Until at last I did arrive
In the Egyptian land.
Wherein that horrid fight
With the fiery dragon bold
Did neither overcome, nor kill,
Nor make my blood run cold.
I fought the cursed dragon and brought him
to the slaughter,
And for that deed did win the King of
Egypt's daughter.
And now the tyrant Valentine
Has challenged me to fight,
And given his word without delay,
To meet me here to-night.
I am for England's right,
And England's admiration,
And soon you'll see me draw
This weapon in vexation.
Is there a man that me can stand?
Let him come, and I'll cut him down
With my courageous hand.

Enter Valentine, the Morocco King, L.

Morocco King: I am the bold Morocco King, and
Valentine is my name;
Thy lofty courage soon my hand
shall turn to shame.
For such a fall thou shalt receive of me;
So let us fight it out most manfully.

6

St. George: Art thou the traitor Valentine,
That led fair Zebedee away,
When I the fiery dragon
For that Egyptian maid did slay?
If thou art he, I'm glad to meet thee here,
And for that thing thy life shall pay most
dear.

Morocco King: St. George, St. George! 'Twere well to
yield thy right,
For lo, I am a King, and thou art but
a knight.

St. George: Oh, thou silly braying ass that feeds on
thistles, weeds, and grass,
Don't offer to abuse a stranger,
For by my word I'll buy a cord
And tie thy nose unto the manger.
None of thy kingly powers do I mind,
My sword shall answer thee and all thy
traitor kind.
Of such a man as thou, I'll never be afraid,
So let us fight it out for the Egyptian maid.

They fight and Valentine is killed.
Enter Prince Imbridge, L.

Imbridge: As I was rising from my bed,
I heard my own dear son was dead.
Oh, thou cursed Christian, what hast thou done?
Thou'st slain me by the slaying of my own dear
son.

St. George: He first to me the challenge gave
And how could I deny, to see how high he
looked
And now how low doth lie?

Imbridge: I see him lying there,
Which makes my heart to bleed;
Distracted I shall run,
Was ever greater need?
Help, help, my faithful Sambo,
Avenge my own dear son.
Make no delay, but gird thyself and take thy
sword in hand,
And fight as a royal subject, under thy King's
command.
For me, my time is come,
For me, my sands are run;
I'll lie me down and die
Along with my own dear son (*Lies down, embraces
Valentine and dies*).

7

Enter Sambo, L.

Sambo: Here come I, Sambo, Prince Imbridge's laws I do
 obey,
 And, with my sword in hand, I hope to win the
 day.
 See, yonder, he that standeth there,
 Hath killed my master and his only son and heir.
 I'll try him if he's made of noble blood,
 I'll make his body flow like Noah's flood.
 I'll through thy body make an empty way
 If thou hast anything against my tender master,
 say.

St. George: I nothing have to say against thy tender
 master or thee,
 So let us fight it out most manfully.

They fight. Sambo is wounded.

Sambo: Hold, hold, St. George, pray fight no more,
 For I am wounded very sore.

St. George: Rise, rise, and speed thee home to thy own
 land,
 And tell what champions thou hast seen
 in old England.

Sambo (*rises*) : I'll rise, St. George, and go my way.
 God bless the King and all his ships at sea.

*Sambo goes out, L. St. George retires, R. Two men remain
lying.*

Enter Dame Dorrity, L.

Dame: Oh, the poor dear men! Oh, the poor dear men!
 (*repeat ad lib.*)
 They've a-been in the wars; they've a-been in the
 wars !

Enter Father Christmas, L.

Father (*singing*)—Fal-the-lal-the-diddle-al-the-day.
 Fal the lal, &c. (*ad lib.*)

Dame: Poor men! They've been in the wars.

Father: In the wars ! in the wars !
 So have I been in the wars ;
 In the battle of pea-soup,
 When the soup flied all over my head,
 And now I'm bald-headed—(*takes off hat*).

Dame: Thee been in the wars ? (*beats him*).
 See these poor dear men (*beats him*).
 I shall get a doctor.

Father: I shall get a carpenter.

Dame: I shall get the doctor.

8

Father : I shall get the carpenter.
They shall have a timmern jacket
That shall last them all their lifetime.

Dame : They shall have a doctor. They ain't dead yet.
Why dissn't feel the pulse of 'em? (*strikes him*).

He lifts Valentine's legs

Father : Here's a fine pair of holds for a sole.

Dame (*beats him*) : Why dissn't feel the pulse of 'em?

He feels their heads

Father : Why their hair is standing like pounds of rushlights.

Dame Dorrity feels pulse

Dame : I'm going for the doctor.

Father : Is there a doctor to be found,
All ready near at hand ;
To cure a deep and deadly wound,
And make these champions stand?

Enter Doctor, R.

Doctor : Oh yes, there is a doctor to be found
All ready near at hand ;
Can cure a deep and deadly wound
And make these champions stand.
I am a learned doctor, lately come from Spain,
I can cure all diseases and raise to life again.
I can cure the itch, the stitch, the palsy, and the
    gout,
And if the devil's in, I'll quickly drive him out.

Father : Thee call he a Spanish doctor? looks more like a
Portugee.

Dame : Insulting the doctor again (*beats him*).
Why dissn't ax him about his fees?

Father (*feels the Doctor's knees*) : Doctor, how's thee knees?

Doctor : What meanest thou? My knees are right.

Mother (*beating him*) : Fees! fees! thee old rogue!

Father : What's fees, fees?

Dame : What's to pay?

Doctor : Ten pounds in money.

Dame : Ten pounds in money!

Father : Ten crocks of honey! I can't carry it.

Dame : Ax him to do it for a farden cheaper.

Father : I am a poor old man, and have a scolding wife.
Cassn't do it for a farden cheaper?

9

Doctor: You're a fatherly looking man,
And have a scolding wife;
And as 'tis such a rogue as thou,
I'll cure them both for five.

Dame: That's the doctor for me; that's the doctor for me.

Father (*beating her*): Go up top a penny loaf and fall
down and break thee neck. That'll be the
doctor for thee.

Dame: Better ax the doctor to get on with his job.
Ax him to give 'em some pills.

Father: Doctor, cassn't thee give 'em some mills?

Doctor: That's what the miller has to grind the corn with.

Dame (*striking him*): Thee old rogue! Why dissn't ax him
for pills?

Father: What dost call they things you stir about in a
bucket?

Dame: Apple dumplings, thee old rogue. That's the bolters
for thee.
(*To doctor*) You'd better go on with your job.

Doctor (*gives pills*). Here's pills to cure ague;
And pills to cure pain;
Here's pills will bring the dead to
life.
Rise, Jack, and fight again.

Both men rise and walk round, arm in arm

Father: Horrible! terrible! the like was never seen;
A man struck out of his seven senses into
nineteen!

*Dance—Father Christmas. Dame Dorrity Doctor, and Valentine
They dance off R.*

Enter Turkish Knight, L.

Turk: Here come I, the Turkish Knight,
Come from the Turkish land to fight.
I'll fight St. George, who is my foe,
I'll make him yield before I go.
He brags to such a high degree,
He thinks there's none the like of he.
So, here I am, the Turkish Knight,
Come from the Turkish land to fight.

Enter St. George, R.

St. George: Fight who?

Turk: Fight thee, St. George, thou man of courage bold,
And if thy blood is hot, I soon will make it cold.

10

St. George: Hold, hold, proud Turk, be not so hot ;
In me is one thou knowest not.
     To whom dost thou the challenge give ?

Turk: To thee, thou English dog !
No longer shalt thou live.

St. George: Talk not of English dog,
    Nor yet of Turkish knight,
    Or in one moment's time
    I'll make thee for to fight.
    Draw forth thy sword and fight,
    Pull out thy purse and pay,
    For satisfaction I will have
    Before thou goest away.

Turk: No satisfaction shalt thou have,
Before I've made of thee my Turkish slave.

They fight. The Turk is struck down.

Turk: Hold, hold, St. George, pray, fight no more,
For I am wounded very sore.

St. George: Rise, rise, thou Turkish dog.
    Go home to thine own land,
    And tell what champions thou hast seen
    In this our old England.
    With 30,000 men like thee I'll fight
    For to maintain the crown which is the
        British right.

Turk (*rises*): I'll rise, St. George, and go my way,
God bless the King, and all his ships at sea.

St. George: Where are my champions, brave ?
Let them appear.

Enter two Mummers, L.

Mummers: Here are thy champions, sword in hand,
Ready to obey at thy command.

St. George: Take that man hence : bind him in chains so
      strong,
Cast him into prison, for his time shall not be
      long.

They take Turk out, L.

St. George: God bless the King and all his men of war,
    Bold British hearts, the soldier and the tar.
    Shades of British heroes, 'gainst whom none
      could stand,
    Now shall rise before us, mighty in command.

11

He waves his sword. Enter Admiral Duncan, R.

Duncan: Drums beat to arms, trumpets sound to fame!
I am a British hero, Admiral Duncan is my name.
I served my Royal Master with credit and renown,
And won for him the victory at the battle of
Camperdown.

St. George waves sword. Enter Lord Nelson, R.

Nelson: Drums beat to arms, trumpets sound to fame!
I am a British hero, Lord Nelson is my name.
On the 26th December, that being the very day,
Nineteen sails of line—some struck, some sunk, some
cowardly bore away.

St. George waves his sword. Enter General Wolfe R

Wolfe: Drums beat to arms, trumpets sound to fame!
I am a British hero, General Wolfe is my name.
How many rocks have I climbéd,
How many walls have I scaléd ?
Never haunted nor daunted at all.
Till at last the fiery bullet
Came and struck me in the gall.
There on the watery sands I bleeding lay,
Midst the fierce sounds of War's alarms,
Till, from above, a Voice to me did say,
Rise, General Wolfe, die in my sheltering arms.

Dance.   All retire, R.

Enter Giant, L

Giant: Here come I, the Giant—'ugh! 'ugh! 'ugh!
Beelzebub's my name—'ugh! 'ugh! 'ugh!
I come here from a giant race.
Is there a man can look me in the face ?
With my long teeth and crooked claws,
Soon will I grind him in my jaws.
Here come I, Beelzebub
Under my arm I carry a club;
Under my chin I carry a pan,
Don't I look a jolly old man ?

Enter Little Man Jan, R.

Jan: Here come I, Little Man Jan,
With sword and pistol in my hand.
Where'er I go they tremble at my sight,
No lord or champion long with me can fight.
I've made the French to tremble and the Spanish for
to quake
I've fought the jolly Dutchmen until their hearts did
ache.
If there's a man will now before me stand,
He soon shall humbly fall by my courageous hand.

*Giant comes forward with a roar. Jan shakes at knees flies round
stage, pursued by Giant. who strikes at Jan and misses.
Jan dodges round, fires pistol, misses, and finally runs out, R.*

12

Enter Slasher. L

Slasher: In come I, Slasher, the Valiant Man.
I dare, Beelzebub, to look thee in the face
And soon will send thee off unto another place.

Giant *(Comes forward with a growl)*:
Who is the daring rogue, who, low or high,
Comes forward with big words me to defy?
I'll beat him and smash him as small as a fly.
And send him to Mother Dorrity to make apple-pie.
I'll grind him and grind him as small as the dust
And sell him to old Father Christmas to make apple-pie
    crust.

Slasher: Oh-ho! I dare thy challenge to defy
And soon thy ugly carcase low at my feet shall lie.

*They fight and dodge round. The Giant hits a tremendous blow
and misses and loses his balance, and Slasher runs him
through. He falls.*

Slasher: *(spurning him)*.
So perish all who dare with me to fight *(retires, L)*.

Enter Father Christmas and Dame Dorrity, R.

Dame: Oh, here's a purty state of things, Oh, my!
Beelzebub's dead.

Father: Then let him die!

Dame *(strikes him)*: You old rogue, don't you see he'll pay
us well if we cure him? Here's more work for the
doctor.

Father: Here's more work for the carpenter. I don't like
the doctor's fees. We owes him five pounds.

Dame: Then charge this man twenty. I'll fetch the doctor.

(Fetches him).

Enter Doctor, R.

Father: Here's a case for some of thy pills
That cures a man of all his deadly ills.
Call this man back to life again
And then of pounds we'll give thee ten.

Dame *(beats him)*: No, no, five. That's the doctor's charge
Now then, doctor, get about it, get about it.

Doctor: Come, take my pills; they cure all ills,
Past, present, and to come.
Take a little of my niff-naff
Put it down thy tiff-taff.
Rise up, and fight again.

Giant *(rises, rubs his eyes)*.
'Tis wondrous strange again to rise
And feel once more the strength that in me lies.

13

Dame: Now. Mr. Beelzebub. you've got to pay the doctor.

Father: Yes, yes, pay the doctor.   I'll take the money.

Giant: How much ?

Father: Twenty pounds in gold.

Doctor: My fee is five.

Dame: He's a rich old gentleman and can pay more ;
It's nought to him to have to pay a score.

Doctor: And what am I to have ?

Dame: You shall have your five.

Father: Yes, you shall have your five and perhaps a farden
more.

Doctor: Not I, forsooth. I'll have the score, or none.

Dame and Father (*striking him*): Then take thee pay in
knocks and get thee gone.

(*They drive him out with blows, R*).

Both (*to Giant*). Now then, the money, the money.

Giant: Best take your pay in knocks, so get you gone
(*drives them out, R*).

Giant: Now will I face St. George or any knight,
Come one, come all, and meet me in my might.

Enter St. George, L.

St. George: To meet thee, swaggering tyrant, I come in.
And over thee the victory will quickly win.

They fight   The Giant is killed. .

St. George: Bearers. this carcase foul at once remove.

St. George retires, L
*Father Christmas, Dame Dorrity. and Mummers enter R, and drag
Giant off L.*

All (*Singing*): Old Jan Page is dead and gone.   Oh, oh, oh !

*Enter L. Tom Bowling with Mummers Father Christmas, and
Dame Dorrity, L.*

Tom Bowling: I'm a jolly, jolly sailor,
Tom Bowling is my name.
Here's me, a man o' war.
Just come ashore,
In hope to beat eleven score.
We'll hoist the guns aboard of them,
And make a terrible noise ;
We'll make the King jump over his
throne,
And all the people shall rejoice.
Cheers. Dance.

14

Tom (*to the others*): Now, who do you think in this ship of
mine
Came over the sea this Christmas time?

Father: Who was it?

Dame (*beats him*): Get thee away, thee inquisitive old rogue'
Here, who com'd over in thee ship?

All gather round Tom Bowling

All: Yes, who was it?

Tom: A champion bold whose name's well known
In this our Minehead town.

All: Come, tell us. Who did you bring?

Tom: King John (*cheers*).
He's lately come from the wars in Spain;
He fought the French with might and main,
But now no longer will he tarry
For he's come back his love to marry.

Father: What! Queen Susan?

First Mummer: A haughty dame! She's waited long;
Methinks for him her love is strong.

Father: I don't think so. I zim she'd think more about
a fine looking feller like me.

Dame (*beats him*): Thee! Why thee'rt allus after the
ladies. I'd like to see her looking at thee.

Father (*beating her*): And thee'rt allus after the men, I tell
thee.

Mummer: Peace, now, and calm your strife.
Here comes the King. Likewise the Queen.
To tarry here might mar their meeting
And gain for us no friendly greeting.
Withdraw (*turns them all out, L*).

Enter King John, R, and Queen Susan. L.

King John: Here come I, King John.

Queen Susan: Here come I, Queen Susan.

King: Madam, to you I bow and bend.

Queen: Stand off, sir, I take you not to be my friend.

King: For why, Madam, did ever I to you do harm?

Queen: Yes, you saucy coxcomb, get you gone.

King: Coxcomb, indeed, is not my name.
Were other lips than thine to say such words,
I'd stab such a saucy dame.

15

Queen: Stab, indeed, is the least I fear,
Appoint a place and I'll meet you there.

King: I'll cross the water at the hour of five,
And meet you there, if I am alive.

Queen: I'll cross the water at the hour of ten,
And meet you there with 20,000 men.

King is going, L.

Why, the man's going, upon my life!

Goes after him.

Stop, stop, sir, do you want a wife?

King: Not such a saucy dame as thou, upon my life!
Why, we'd tipple and nipple over an orange.

Queen: Such trivial things with us shall not make strife.

King: Fair dame, I think a fickle mind thou hast,
But, loving thee, I'll fearless take the chance

(takes hold round her).

So we'll appoint the day of marriage.
Music play up merrily, and we will have a dance.

Dance.

Duet :—

King: Long time I courted you, miss,
I'm just returned from sea,
We'll make no more to do, miss.
But quickly married be.
Sing ri-fal-the-diddle-al-the-dee,
Ri-fal-the-diddle-al-the-day.

Queen: I never did wed a tar, sir,
Deceitful as yourself.
It's very plain, you are, sir
A good-for-nothing elf.
Sing ri-fal, &c.

King: It's useless to contend, miss,
So let the storm subside;
Our courtship's at an end, miss,
Thou ne'er shall be my bride.
Sing ri-fal, &c.

Queen: False man, you courted Sally,
With vows you filled her head.
And Susan of the valley,
You promised her you'd wed.
Sing ri-fal, &c.

16

King : Now, dearest girl, surrender.

Queen : Yes, love, I'll be your wife;

King : And I'll be your defender,

Queen : And I'll be true for life.

Sing, ri-fal, &c. Dance.

Enter Mummers.

Mummers : Music, play up merrily.

Song, during which the various characters enter, beginning with St. George.

Music merrily play,
  And cannons loudly roar,
You're welcome home, St. George,
  Home to your native shore.
    You're welcome, &c.

Oh, the next we do call in,
  It is our noble King;
He's lately come from the war,
  Glad tidings he doth bring,
    He's lately, &c.

Oh, the next we do call in,
  It is the Squire's son,
It's all because of his love,
  Because he was so young.
    It's all because, &c.

Although I've been in the wars,
  It's not for any harm;
It's all for the sake of my love,
  Because I was so young.
    It's all because, &c.

Oh, divers is the next,
  And misers you shall see;
In spending all their gold,
  Now they're come to poverty.
    In spending, &c.

Hodge-bodge, I have forgot,
  He's one of all our crew;
And if I must tell you plain,
  My dear, I'm in love with you.
    And if I must tell, &c

Oh, music, change your tunes,
  And play right merrily,
That we may have a dance,
  For to please our company.
    That we may have, &c.

Dance—Finale.

A snow-bound Minehead from Church Steps.

Christmas at Allerford

From *Two Admirals*, 1909

JOHN MORESBY, BORN IN ALLERFORD IN 1830

The village worked and slept until Christmas brought the high tide and holiday of the year. Anxiously we children listened for the thundering knock at the door which announced the mummers, when, in answer to our scream of 'Who's there?' would come the masculine chorus:

> Here come I, old Father Christmas!
> Christmas or not,
> I hope old Father Christmas
> Will never be forgot.

It certainly would not by us. We tore the door open, and in marched a medley of villagers, armed with wooden swords, paper helmets, and ribbons streaming from their smocks – a glorious, jovial sight. Immediately St George stood forth – the majesty of England incarnate – and challenged the Turkish knight to deadly combat, whilst breathless we watched the fight until he fell before St George's conquering sword. There was a pause full of awe for us, and then the victor demanded in the epic strain that befits heroes:

> Is there a doctor that can be found
> To cure this knight of his deadly wound?
> (accentuating the rhymes of 'found' and 'wound').

There was. The doctor, smock-frocked and rosy, stood forth and declared with all the confidence of his profession.

> I'll touch his eyes, his mouth and chin,
> And say, 'Rise, dead man, and fight agin!'

It was done; the resurrection was completed with a few whacking blows, and our feelings were relieved accordingly. Then cider and sixpences followed, and the singing of the old Somerset and Devon ballads – 'Widdicombe Fair' and the like – until, with a final cheer for my parents, the mummers departed to awake the village echoes on their devious way home.

We children had Exmoor ponies, which we rode bare-backed as we galloped over the moors. With a bent pin baited with caddis we landed miraculous catches of minnows, and sometimes even a trout, from the myriad waters of that land of streams. But the Christmas coming of the Aclands at Holnicote was the purple patch of our year. There we all fore-gathered, young and old, round the wood fire in the hall where on Christmas Eve lay the Yule log – an ashen faggot bound with seven withy bands – and as each band cracked and snapped in the flame, with clapping of hands and infinite rejoicing we each wished a wish.

Later the custom, descending from heathen times, of wassailing the apple-trees was faithfully observed. Every old gun, blunderbuss, or pistol that the village could produce was brought out, and masters and men, women and children, all trooped to the principal orchard, the men with their guns, the women with wassail-bowls filled with cider hot and spiced, and bobbing with roasted apples. Then, with shouting and cheering and a general *feu de joie* over the trees, all joined in the chorus:

> Old apple-tree, I wassail thee,
> And well mayst thou bear
> Hats full, caps full, rooms full,
> For cider bright and fair.

Finally, a piece of bread soaked in cider was left on the branches of a tall apple-tree.

Pyles Mill, Allerford.

Winter Solstice
1982

The cold hangs like a pall over the earth.
In the dyke bottom, safe from sleet and wind,
Misled by the foreshadowing of night
Into a premature forsaking of its harassed search
Beneath each frosted frond, each lisping wand,
Roosting uneasily, dissatisfied, at half-past three,
A listless rail pecks vainly at its breath
That floats like a plucked blossom on the dry stalks
Of the sedge.

A shrunken child now threads his muffled way
Along a footpath that his fathers knew;
From bright schoolroom appearing
And into misty gloom soon soundless fading
As did they. Scant sun has been all day;
A rusty sky beyond the apple tree
The only evidence. Full coated cattle
Wait, haloed in steam, for milking call.

All busyness, all liveliness succumbs
While the still ploughshares rest on the slabbed row.
The reeking tractor plods with sluggish oil,
And calloused palms turn from the kiss of iron
With its numb lips to kindliness of wood.
The hedger stirs the embers with his tool,
Straightening his back to see the sullen sparks
Leap low, fall slow this homing time.

Old Time Revels (New Year's Eve)

From *Exmoor Lyrics and Other Verses*, 1910

ROSE E. SHARLAND

Now heave the ash faggot and pile on the fire
To build up the dying year's funeral pyre.
See the blaze leap and run seething along,
Hear the wild flames hiss their sibilant song!
What matter though Boreas thunder without?
The gladness within shall put winter to rout.
So who 's for the ingle-nook? Nance shall go in
Nearest the fire till the revels begin,
Prison her there till the fierce-glowing heat
Soon makes her long for a cooler retreat.
Pretty cheeks burning, she barters for peace,
Wooing red lips begging speedy release,
That must be paid for – a kiss, perhaps two,
Blue eyes flash lightnings! The captive breaks through!
Skirmish around the old kitchen, and now
Capture and truce 'neath the mistletoe bough.

Tune up the fiddle! In measured tones slow
Sing of the good looks of 'Billy Barlow;'
Then to the merrier trip of the reel
Rollicking strains to the low rafters peal,
Telling of how, on a star-shiny night,
Walks through the glades are a poacher's delight.
Then Gaffer Ridler in quaking tones sings
Old Devon folk-songs of courting and rings,

Quaint rhyming medleys, where parsons and brides
Mingle with wrestling-bouts, cross-country rides,
Feastings and jollity, cheeses and ale,
Cider and cream in a weird, rhythmic tale.
After each verse all the party join in,
Vying each other in jubilant din.
Grandfather, cheered by the laughter and joy,
Leads off a dance he had learned as a boy.
To his dim eyes comes awhile the old light,
Thinking of some far-away old year's night,
When, envied much by the whole country-side,
He set the step with his sweet blushing bride.
Still the same measure! It rings out again,
Oh, but the wonderful changes since then!
'Over the water and over the lea,
Over the water to Charlie.'
Now Nance is tripping with handsome young Ned
Just the same dance as the dancers long dead.

Come, crouch round the embers, and fill up the bowl,
This is the magic the past to unroll!
Hast heard of Moll Arnold, the witch of the wood,
She who could change to a hare when she would?
Whisper the story in low, bated breath;
How she was chased in a hunt that meant death,
Up through the wood, till no woman was seen,
Only a black hare far over the green
Tell how she bore bramble marks on her face,
When the next morn through the old marketplace,
Bringing her milk from her cottage she came;
Even now voices grow soft at her name.
Hear how her magic on Uncle Jan fell,
Three horses died by her horrible spell,
One of their hearts was hung over the fire,
So, as it charred, should the witch-craft expire.
Later old uncle himself was bewitched

(Some said his barns by her powers were enriched),
For he fell ill and grew rapidly worse,
Till one black night he got rid of the curse,
Taking some nails and a hammer around,
He drove through her foot-print the spell to the ground.
What latest pranks by the pixies is played?
Young Farmer Endacott's man was waylaid.
Last Christmas Eve he was pixy-led sure,
Spent all night long wandering up on the moor,
Nor, when he got to his home, could he say
What had befallen him late yesterday!
Look! Gran is sleeping! Waken her up,
Drink to the past in a jovial cup!
Tickle her nose with a feather and say,
'None must be snoring the old year away.'
Five minutes left! Now the hush-spell is cast,
Gran and the old folk are back in the past,
Nance and the boys see a wonderful Spring
Casting love-gladness on everything,
Age hanging on to the years that are dead,
Youth glad enough of another year sped.
Silence! Suspense! Then the grandfather clock
Groans out its knell. There's a turn of the lock,
Rush of chill air as the slow hinges spin –
Bob from the farm lets the new-born year in!

The North Wind Doth Blow...

From *Wild Harvest*, 1978

HOPE BOURNE

Winter brings frost and ice, and snow, though not usually until after Christmas. Frost when it comes sets the ground like concrete and all waters save the fast-running streams turn to ice. Since I do not like a stuffy bedroom and always sleep with the window open, letting the stove out when I go to bed, the temperature of the interior of my tiny little home drops by dawn to that of the outer air, and commonly when I wake-up everything that can freeze is frozen stiff – the water bucket almost solid ice, the lids of kettle and tea-pot frozen on, eggs (if I've got any) split with the cold, and, if I have not remembered to drain my flower-jug before turning-in, that will be split too (I've lost several favourite vases that way) whilst often the hoar-frost sparkles on the walls and ceiling. However, a quickly-made fire and a boiling kettle soon warm things up. The simplest way of unfreezing the water in the bucket is to heat the flat-iron and stand on the ice! (Some folk shudder at the thought of such an awakening, but I am myself convinced that this Spartan living is one of the reasons I never have coughs, colds, or other ills.) And once out of doors, it's dry and usually gloriously sunny as the morning advances!

Snow is something no one looks forward to in these parts, for when it comes it is usually in the form of fierce blizzards, and this is sheep-country and sheep are most vulnerable in heavy snow. As to what snow can be like in this country, well, I have many memories of many blizzards. Snow whirling like blind white smoke, snow driving in horizontal sheets, thick as a wall, on a wind so bitter that neither sheep nor cattle will face it, drifts mounting high as gateways, high as hedges, high as roofs. Lanes filled-in to the tops of their banks, sheep buried, tractors buried, snow-ploughs buried. Telegraph poles snapped-off at their roots and flung across the moor in a welter of wires. Days of desparate digging, digging out sheep, digging out gateways, digging out doorways. Days of struggle to feed the beasts, days of being cut-off from the rest of the world. Days followed by nights so bitter that the dung freezes to the shippon floor as it drops. Every farm so cut-off must fend for itself and look to its own needs without hope of outside help. Wise folk will have good stores of food-stuffs for man and beast and a good woodpile in the yard before the onset of winter, and come to no harm. Myself, I always lay-in 'iron rations' sufficient for four months, just before Christmas (not that one expects snow to last that long – but it did in '63).

The hazards of Snow are many, from getting lost in a blinding blizzard, being smothered in fresh drifts, collapsing from exhaustion on open ground, to being chopped by a mass of snow suddenly descending from shippon roofs as it thaws. (The weight of packed snow is something you believe when you have been hit by some of it.) No-one but a fool goes beyond the shelter of hedge-banks in a blizzard, nor out at all except to see to the safety of beasts. Some there are who have died because of foolhardiness.

Something too, not always realized, is that snow drifts on the lee side of hedges and walls – that is why sheep bury, seeking shelter from the blast.

One thing, though, one can never be short of in deep snow, is water! It has come as a great surprise to me to hear folk say sometimes they have been in sore straights for water because their plumbing has frozen-up. Well, one bucket full of snow renders down to a third of water very quickly, so you can't really die of thirst!

In time of snow, do not go out in a blizzard unless you absolutely have to, and once the stuff is down, don't blunder into fresh snowdrifts. They are too soft to bear your weight, and you will go in – perhaps ten feet or more and may get smothered. If the snowfall is very deep, stay near home for three weeks, by which time the drifts will have 'packed' under their own weight and you can walk over the top of them. And always carry a spade with you, so that you can dig yourself through or out of an awkward place. Also remember snow sliding off roofs has force enough to break your back.

When bitter frost binds the earth to iron, beware of skidding on patches of ice or wrenching an ankle in the frozen hoof-holes. About home, spread ashes or loose hay on the paths where you walk the most – else these soon become like skating-rinks.

Most of all perhaps you need to keep your wits about you when feeding livestock, particularly cattle, in mid-winter. They are ravenous, poor creatures, and on foot and alone it is difficult to keep them at bay whilst you carry and spread the hay for them. Apart from being directly pushful, they are apt to charge each other out of frustration, and in doing so may knock you down. Being trampled on by a herd of bullocks isn't a nice thought.

So, having learned, as I've said, to differentiate between a calculated, necessary risk and a stupid unnecessary one, I just remember that famous British saying: 'Trust in God and keep your powder dry'.

The Great Freeze

J.M. SLADER, 1963

The winter of 1962-63 was exceptional, even in a twentieth century that experienced the devastating cold spells of 1940 and 1947. The 1963 Exmoor Review *contained a number of pieces recording the event, including a first-hand account of hill-farming under terrible conditions by Brian Duke and an historical survey of the worst winter seasons by J.M. Slader. It is appropriate to place in between them the most famous version of an Exmoor blizzard – R.D. Blackmore's, from* Lorna Doone.

The winter of 1963 will be remembered even a century from now as man compares his weather in the mid-21st century with records of bygone years.

The Westcountry blizzards, the marooned villages, the isolated farmsteads, the railway engines unable to complete their journeys, the abandoned cars, the sheep and ponies desperate for the essentials that sustain life will be recalled even then.

Upon Exmoor history records several similar great winters 1607, 1615, 1676, 1740, 1776, 1814, 1895 and 1947. How differently, though, we survive such conditions to-day. The friendly helicopters, their heroic crews striving against almost impossible conditions to relieve the sick, to feed the animals, to supply the daily bread. The clearing of snowdrifts by mechanical means. Light and warmth at the turn of the switch, the refrigerator and deep freeze stocked to forestall the siege. Aid and attention at the end of the telephone; frozen meat, vegetables and groceries down at the village shop.

Just think of life upon the moor in those merciless winters of old. The isolated farmhouse, lit by oil and candle. The only way to reach civilisation at Minehead, Lynton, South Molton, or Dulverton was to walk. No radio, television, no weather bulletin to warn of what was to come. Villages and hamlets were not just isolated for days but for weeks, the deep lanes filled to the hedgetops, the great drifts cutting the turnpikes. The countryside came to a standstill, and even in the towns, shops and businesses shut their doors until the warm air and sunshine came once again. Markets were closed, the inns surrounding the high moor, unable to replenish their supplies, closed their doors. The cold unheated churches shut down their services; the children, those that were fortunate to attend school, were given long holidays. Poverty and unem-ployment were rife.

Many of the Exmoor farmers of the eighteenth and nineteenth centuries failed to survive such a winter. Even the large landowners took many years to recover.

The old Exmoor farmers' notebooks which have been handed down to us give many instances of the havoc that was wrought. 1607 – 'About a fortnight before Christmas' (Christmas was not then celebrated on December 25th but on what is now January 5th, and in order to fall into line with the Continental calendar, 11 days were cut right out) 'began the hard frost and snow, which continued about five weeks; victuals were frozen so hard that they would take no salt; the cold meat kept over night was so hard that it could not be cut to be eaten – for I had a piece of beef roasted on New Year's Day and kept and then I was driven to take a spit and put the end thereof in the fire and heat it red hot and so got him to the flesh.' 1676 – 'The frost is recorded so great that the oldest man living did never know the like for everything was so hard that meat could only be roasted; because they could get no water for to boyle the pot.' Another source records the Exmoor winter of 1615 as lasting from January 16th to May 20th.

In *Lorna Doone* R. D. Blackmore dates 'The Great Winter' as 1686. This cannot be verified from local records, but it is generally assumed that the author meant the winter of 1676. This is the greatest available description of a severe Exmoor winter of olden times, supposedly passed down to Blackmore from his great-grandfather's grandfather, who witnessed the winter from the ancestral farmstead of Bodley, in the parish of Parracombe. 'That night such a frost ensued as we had never dreamed of, neither read in ancient books, or histories of Frobisher. The kettle by the fire froze, and the crock upon the hearth-cheeks ; many men were killed, and cattle rigid in their head-ropes.'

The most interesting diary to come to light in recent years is that of John Thorne, of North Radworthy, in the parish of North Molton. Here this 'caretaker of the soil' farmed these bleak acres upon the edge of the moor for nearly forty years, taking over upon the death of his father in 1790.

Of the winter of 1814 he writes: 'The terriblest winter this year ever since that one in 1776, that is thirty-eight years ago. Began the 6th day of January, snow and three or four snows else, then a day's rain and froze to the ground, bushes, trees, hedges, broke them all down with the weight, which was two and three inches thick in some places of ice. Then before it broke away it snowed two nights and most two days with a tempest of wind that blowed the snow in the biggest drifts ever known. The ice lay on the ground for more than a week. Many sheep under snow, 29 Shortecombe and nine of them dead. Forced to take in every sheep from Shortecombe in the in-ground and give them hay.'

'There was not a sheep on the Darlicks, Shortecombe Easter and Wester Butterys, all forced to take them in and give them hay by reason of the ice, that they could not taste a bit of grass, twig or furze nor anything, for the furze and wood and hedges was all bowed down with the ice and then covered with overwhelming snow. Forced to give hay to the Exmore colts and other colts. Go to mill on foot. No horse could go, the drifts were so high, forced to go over the fields, the roads mostly full, it were eight snows, it hold most five weeks.'

This was the winter of the last Frost Fair, held upon the frozen Thames, above the old London Bridge, and one that much resembles those of 1947 and 1963. Such winters, unpleasant though they may be, take their place in history and will be remembered long after we pass from this earthly scene.

Nature can no longer ruin a prosperous farm within a few months of severe winter weather. The Exmoor farmers, their employees, and all those who live within the bounds of this beautiful region must surely be thankful to modern methods of agriculture, mechanisation, and everything that this century of industrial and scientific progress has brought us.

The Big Freeze of 1962-63, Molland.

The Great Exmoor Snow

From *Lorna Doone*, 1869

R.D. BLACKMORE

It must have snowed most wonderfully to have made that depth of covering in about eight hours. For one of Master Stickles' men, who had been out all the night, said that no snow began to fall until nearly midnight. And here it was, blocking up the doors, stopping the ways, and the watercourses, and making it very much worse to walk than in a saw-pit newly used. However we trudged along in a line; I first, and the other men after me; trying to keep my track, but finding legs and strength not up to it. Most of all, John Fry was groaning; certain that his time was come, and sending messages to his wife, and blessings to his children. For all this time it was snowing harder than it ever had snowed before, so far as a man might guess at it; and the leaden depth of the sky came down, like a mine turned upside down on us. Not that the flakes were so very large; for I have seen much larger flakes in a shower of March, while sowing peas; but that there was no room between them, neither any relaxing, nor any change of direction.

Watch, like a good and faithful dog, followed us very cheerfully, leaping out of the depth, which took him over his back and ears already, even in the level places; while in the drifts he might have sunk to any distance out of sight, and never found his way up again. However, we helped him now and then, especially through the gaps and gateways; and so after a deal of floundering, some laughter and a little swearing, we came all safe to the lower meadow, where most of our flock was hurdled.

But behold, there was no flock at all! None, I mean, to be seen anywhere; only at one corner of the field, by the eastern end, where the snow drove in, a great white billow, as high as a barn and as broad as a house. This great drift was rolling and curling beneath the violent blast, tufting and combing with rustling swirls, and carved (as in patterns of cornice) where the grooving chisel of the wind swept round. Ever and again, the tempest snatched little whifis from the channelled edges, twirled them round, and made them lie like herring-bones, or the seams of sand where the tide had been. And all the while from the smothering sky, more and more fiercely at every blast, came the pelting pitiless arrows, winged with murky white, and pointed with the barbs of frost.

But although, for people who had no sheep, the sight was a very fine one (so far at least as the weather permitted any sight at all); yet for us, with our flock beneath it, this great mount had but little charm. Watch began to scratch at once, and to howl along the sides of it; he knew that his charge was buried there, and his business taken from him. But we four men set to in earnest, digging with all our might and main, shovelling away at the great white pile, and fetching it into the meadow. Each man made for himself a cave, scooping at the soft cold flux, which slid upon him at every stroke, and throwing it out behind him, in piles of castled fancy. At last we drove our tunnels in (for we worked indeed for the lives of us), and all converging towards the middle, held our tools and listened.

The other men heard nothing at all; or declared that they heard nothing, being anxious now to abandon the matter, because of the chill in their feet and knees. But I said, 'Go, if you choose, all of you. I will work it out by myself, you pie-crusts.' And upon that they gripped their shovels, being more or less of Englishmen; and the least drop of English blood is worth the best of any other, when it comes to lasting out.

But before we began again, I laid my head well into the chamber; and there I heard a faint 'ma-a-ah,' coming through some ells of snow, like a plaintive buried hope, or a last appeal. I shouted aloud to cheer him up, for I knew what sheep it was, to wit the most valiant of all the wethers, who had met me when I came home from London and been so glad to see me. And then we all fell to again; and very soon we hauled him out. Watch took charge of him at once, with an air of the noblest patronage, lying on his frozen fleece; and licking all his face and feet, to restore his warmth to him. Then fighting Tom jumped up at once, and made a little butt at Watch, as if nothing had ever ailed him, and then set off to a shallow place, and looked for something to nibble at.

Further in, and close under the bank, where they had huddled themselves for warmth, we found all the rest of the poor sheep packed as closely as if they were in a great pie. It was strange to observe how their vapour, and breath, and the moisture exuding from their wool had scooped, as it were, a coved room for them, lined with a ribbing of deep yellow snow. Also the churned snow beneath their feet was as yellow as gamboge. Two or three of the weaklier hoggets were dead, from want of air, and from pressure; but more than three-score were as lively as ever; though cramped and stiff for a little while.

'However shall us get 'em home?' John Fry asked in great dismay, when we had cleared about a dozen of them; which we were forced to do very carefully, so as not to fetch the roof down. 'No manner of maning to draive 'un, drough all they girt driftnesses.'

'You see to this place; John,' I replied, as we leaned on our shovels a moment, and the sheep came rubbing round us: 'let no more of them out for the present; they are better where they be. Watch, here boy, keep them!'

Watch came, with his little scut of a tail cocked as sharp as duty; and I set him at the narrow mouth of the great snow antre. All the sheep sidled away, and got closer, that the other sheep might be bitten first, as the foolish things imagine: whereas no good sheep-dog even so much as lips a sheep to turn it.

Then of the outer sheep (all now snowed and frizzled like a lawyer's wig) I took the two finest and heaviest, and with one beneath my right arm, and the other beneath my left, I went straight home to the upper sheppey, and set them inside, and fastened them. Sixty and six I took home in that way, two at a time on each journey; and the work grew harder and harder each time, as the drifts of the snow were deepening. No other man should meddle with them: I was resolved to try my strength against the strength of the elements; and try it I did, ay and proved it. A certain fierce delight burned in me, as the struggle grew harder; but rather would I die than yield; and at last I finished it. People talk of it to this day: but none can tell what the labour was, who have not felt that snow and wind.

Of the sheep upon the mountain, and the sheep upon the western farm, and the cattle on the upper burrows, scarcely one in ten was saved; do what we would for them. And this was not through any neglect (now that our wits were sharpened), but from the pure impossibility of finding them at all. That great snow never ceased a moment for three days and nights; and then when all the earth was filled, and the topmost hedges were unseen, and the trees broke down with weight (wherever the wind had not lightened them), a brilliant sun broke forth and showed the loss of all our customs.

All our house was quite snowed up, except where we had purged a way, by dint of constant shovellings. The kitchen was as dark and darker than the cider-cellar, and long lines of furrowed scallops ran even up to the chimney-stacks. Several windows fell right inwards, through the weight of the snow against them; and the few that stood bulged in, and bent like an old bruised lanthorn. We were obliged to cook by candlelight; we were forced to read by candlelight; as for baking, we could not do it, because the oven was too chill; and a load of faggots only brought a little wet down the sides of it.

For when the sun burst forth at last upon that world of white, what he brought was neither warmth, nor cheer, nor hope of softening; only a clearer shaft of cold, from the violet depths of sky. Long-drawn alleys of white haze seemed to lead towards him, yet such as he could not come down, with any warmth remaining. Broad white curtains of the frost-fog looped around the lower sky, on the verge of hill and valley, and above the laden trees. Only round the sun himself, and the spot of heaven he claimed, clustered a bright purple-blue, clear, and calm, and deep.

That night, such a frost ensued as we had never dreamed of, neither read in ancient books, or histories of Frobisher. The kettle by the fire froze, and the crock upon the hearth-cheeks; many men were killed, and cattle rigid in their head-ropes. Then I heard that fearful sound, which never I had heard before, neither since have heard (except during that same winter), the sharp yet solemn sound of trees, burst open by the frost-blow. Our great walnut lost three branches, and has been dying ever since; though growing meanwhile, as the soul does. And the ancient oak at the cross was rent, and many score of ash trees. But why should I tell all this? the people who have not seen it (as I have) will only make faces, and disbelieve; till such another frost comes; which perhaps may never be.

Winter at Warren Farm

BRIAN DUKE, 1963

On Christmas Eve, as there were signs of snow, my father and I turned our sheep, which were on the high ground about Larkbarrow, Toms Hill, Pinford, and Trout Hill, two hundred and fifty down in the Kittuck Valley and seven hundred and fifty to the bottom of Manor Allotment and Deer Park. This is our usual practice, as they are unlikely to bury there. Besides these breeding ewes there were three hundred hogs. They were here around Warren Farm.

It was on Boxing Day that the first fall of snow came. This blocked our road and we were cut off. It was on December 29th, however, that the first real fall of snow came with huge drifts. We had about seventy hogs (last year's lambs) buried, but managed to dig them all out safely that day; but it was impossible to reach our ewes, although we made some attempts. Snow was waist deep. On New Year's Day Mr J. Hayes, Manager of the Fortescue Estates, with an estate workman, walked out with bread, etc., and wanted to know if we wanted anything. On the following Sunday Mr Hayes and the same workman arrived again early in the morning, and it was arranged to walk to Kittuck, so the four of us set off. Crossing Hayes Allotment was very difficult because the snow was still soft and there was a very thick fog. We managed to find the hedge and walked along that to Larkbarrow Corner, straight on to Larkbarrow Road Gate, and from there the entire length of the hedge bordering Porlock Common. We reached Kittuck about 2.30 to find the sheep in good condition. Hay had been dropped to them earlier in the week by a helicopter from Chivenor.

On 8th January our telephone was repaired. In the evening it was arranged (by telephone) that an attempt should be made to get the sheep home from Kittuck. We were fortunate enough to be able to get a helicopter. At Simonsbath it picked up two shepherds, Denzil Curtis and Russell Hicks, and a dog, and then came on here. It landed up in a field about 200 yards from the house, where it picked up my father and I and another dog. We reached Kittuck at about half-past ten and then we had the rest of the day to get the sheep home. Although the snow was a little harder, it was still very soft in places. My father went on ahead with about 12 sheep to make a path, and the other three of us each brought on a bunch behind. We were able to go over gates and hedges as the snow was quite hard here. We arrived home safely at about 3.30. It would have been impossible to have done this in one day had it not been for the helicopter.

The following day we met Mr Hayes up on Honeymead Allotment and sent the 50 Galloway cows which we have here back to Simonsbath as we were getting rather short of fodder. On 12th January my father and I walked to Manor Allotment, here again using a very roundabout way walking along on the hedges. These sheep, too, were in good condition, hay had also been dropped to these on several occasions. During the next few days we walked to Manor Allotment two or three times a week. On 14th January a bulldozer from Honeymead started to clear the

Cornham Brake, Simonsbath.

E.R.J. Davey

road, and three days later a tractor was able to get in with various supplies. A couple of days later I was able to ride over to Honeymead to fetch meat and mail which had been left there.

During the next weeks we continued walking to Manor Allotment, then on February 4th we decided to bring home a bunch. The difficulty was to get them home. The sheep had to come up over the Forest, and this was very hard going. However, we managed it. There were 477 on Manor Allotment and this was the bunch we brought home. On the following evening, 5th February, it began blowing a gale and snow falling very fast. This was a vile night and proved to be the worst of the winter. We had about 900 sheep in the farmyard that night and the snow was drifting so badly that we stayed up most of the night to stop them burying. In the morning my father was able to touch the snow out of his bedroom window.

The next few days followed a slow thaw and our road was cleared part way. From there we and three other men carried hay on our backs up to the farm. Snow fell again through the week-end and on Monday, 11th February, a helicopter dropped some coal to us. It landed on a very small spot just in front of the house. This had been arranged by Mr Hayes and Mr Holman. Mr and Mrs Holman had their hotel as a distribution centre in the village, and everyone was very grateful to them.

On February 12th my father walked to the other end of the Deer Park to see another bunch of sheep, and the next day he and two other men walked out and brought them home. Our road had been cleared earlier in the week enough for a tractor to get in, and the snow became quite hard; in fact, I was able to ride my pony over the tops of gates and hedges without even seeing them. One day I rode from here to the other end of Deer Park (almost down to Cloud Farm) over the top of the drifts.

It was on March 5th that the long-awaited thaw really got under way and the snow was shifting very fast. On Thursday, 7th March, our road was sufficiently clear for us to get out with our van. This was the first time it had been out since 23rd December – 74 days. There was still snow on Manor Allotment on May 4th, 129 days after Boxing Day.

Night Over the High Moor

JUDITH SMALLSHAW, 1979

Deep in the poverty of winter
ponies stand
knee-deep in coppered bracken.
Grey-golden, the lichen spirals
over fallen trees
and, filigreed with frost,
the brown, unstirring leaves
hang by winter's chain.
Sodden moss, clinging
to the little marshy places,
is briefly grooved
by a single red deer's cloven step.

Brittle with stars,
the night is drenched with timelessness:
a dog fox pauses, listening;
an owl
touches the silent substance of the sky
... and the land lies passionless,
her matted heather cloak
wrapped close against the dark.

The Depths of Winter

From *A Moorland Year*, 1993

HOPE BOURNE

Glass frost. One step outside my door and I go down on the flat of my back with the soles of my feet up to heaven. The next thing is to get up. Easier said than done. Each attempt results in going down whack again. However, I do at last get back indoors and then re-emerge with a panfull of fire-ash to strew in front of my feet, and so cross the skating-rink that is the yard and get to the barn where the tools lie. Then, digger in hand, I set out to chop little paths in the ice-sheet to wherever I need to go.

Gradually I work my way out onto the Ball and look around. The whole world roundabout is one of dazzling white frozen snow, shining and glistening like a polished mirror in the morning sun. The ground is sheet-ice, the branches of trees, and all things projecting above ground level, are coated to many times their own thickness with glittering ice as though molten glass had been poured over them. I call the sheep, as I have a bag of cake for them, and they come, or try to come, stiff-legged as though they were on skates. This way and that they skid, tobogganing and colliding on the glasslike surface. The dodgems at Barnstaple Fair come a good second!

On the way back I make an error: a sideways step to look into the combe. My feet are gone from me and I am skidding down the precipitous slope on my back! Faster and faster, and I know there's a line of withies at the bottom by the stream. If I crack against them at the speed I'm going, I'll do myself an injury. Desperately I manage to roll over and try to clutch at whatever protrudes – gorse and brambles and the like – above the ice, and manage to come to a reasonable stop by the withies. Next, how do I get back up? Directly is impossible so I work my way down the combe till I meet the junction with the lane, then haul myself homewards by the hedge. Am thankful to be back with a mug of hot tea in my hands!

Glass frost can occur in one of two ways: a partial thaw after snow, followed by a sudden severe frost (as now) or by heavy rain suddenly freezing. I have known both, and in the latter case, many years ago now, sheep were frozen to the ground and had to be helped up.

Blizzard. For three days and three nights the snow has come out of the east on a howling wind. It comes now with terrible elemental force, battering, blinding, tearing, choking, the sky is gone, the moor is blotted out, there is nothing but snow between heaven and earth.

Trees and hedges bend before the fury. Wherever there is a gap or gateway, the snow blows through in great white clouds. Everywhere the drifts mount up and up, smoking at the tops like volcanos. Up to the hedges, over the gates, up to the eves of buildings, over the shoulders of combes. Every hollow is filled, every lane choked to the top of its banks. And still it snows.

I stay close to the buildings, carrying a spade to dig my way where I must, then move along to the lee-side of the hedge-banks to get to the small field at the back of the barn where the ewes abide. They are huddled in the middle, heads and backs above the snow. Hopefully they will stay there and not bury. They have the windbreak of three tall beech hedges which should hold back the full force of the blizzard somewhat. The danger is if they draw too much to the shelter of the lee-side, for it is here, by the bitter irony of Nature, that the drifts grow deepest and highest, it is here that sheep bury.

I am glad to come down again, back to the life-saving comfort of home and warmth. It is like the return to port from a ferocious sea. Beyond the enclosing harbour of walls and windbreaks the storm is impossible to face. It comes at you like a moving wall of white. You cannot see through it, cannot look into it. It cuts off your breath with its icy cold and stifles you. You cannot walk, the ever-mounting snow muffles your feet. Woe to the traveller lost on the moor, all land marks gone. Some there are who have not come home.

Where are all the wild things now? Where are the ponies? All things must struggle to survive, how they can, if they can. The ponies like the deer will live, they know where to find shelter enough, how to pick at any vegetation that protrudes above the snow. The lesser creatures, alas, so very many will die. That any will survive at all – as a few always do – seems a miracle.

I do the little that I can. I beat down patches of snow by my door, and crumble and spread whatever I can spare of foodstuff for the birds (and the hayseed from the bales helps too). So many come. Blackbirds, robins, tits, chaffinches, dunnocks, starlings and a handsome cock-pheasant as well. The tiny wrens make my heart ache. They will not pick at the crumbs, or the hayseeds that help the other birds, though they fly into the barn in the hope of insects in the crevices.

Beyond this, I can only pray, for myself, the animals and the birds, and hope the blizzard will blow itself out soon.

Acknowledgements

Hilary Binding has offered indispensable guidance and assistance throughout the preparation of this volume and it could not have been completed without her help.

I am grateful to her in her capacity as editor of the *Exmoor Review* and to the Exmoor Society for permission to reproduce the following :

'The Great Freeze' by J. M. Slader, *Exmoor Review*, 1963
'Winter at Warren Farm' by Brian Duke, *Exmoor Review*, 1963
'Exmoor at Christmas' by Maureen Hosegood, *Exmoor Review*, 1967
'Winter on an Exmoor Farm' by Alice R. Elliott, *Exmoor Review*, 1970
'The Village School in Winter' by Cicely Cooper, *Exmoor Review*, 1979
'Night Over the High Moor' by Judith Smallshaw, *Exmoor Review*, 1979
'Winter Solstice' *Exmoor Review*, 1982

I am also indebted to : Anne Williamson and the Henry Williamson Literary Estate for permission to reproduce the excerpt from *The Linhay on the Downs* by Henry Williamson; to Berta Lawrence, Hope Bourne, Glyn Court, and Brian Pearce, whom it has been my pleasure to publish over the years; to Michael Deering, creator of the Exmoor Photographic Archive, and to Brenda Massie, its custodian; and to David Bromwich and Liz Clark of the Somerset Studies Library. To them all I offer my thanks and the Compliments of the Season.